CONQUERING
CYNICISM IN A MODERN AGE

For comments or questions about this book,
visit our website: *The Lost Stories Channel*, at
loststorieschannel.com

© 2023 by W. Kent Smith – All Rights Reserved
Published in the United States by
Lodestar Cinema Creations,
in association with Staten House
West Covina, California
Smith, W. Kent (1959-)

Front Cover and Title Page Painting:
Diogenes in Search of a Man,
Pieter van Mol, 1645

Book Exterior and Interior
Designed and Executed
by W. Kent Smith

All the artwork for this book is in the public domain and is therefore not subject to copyright infringement.

No part of this book may be reproduced in any form without the prior written consent of the publisher, except in brief quotations embodied in critical articles and reviews.

ISBN: 979-8-90148-560-6

Manufactured in the U.S.A.
September 2023

Conquering
Cynicism in a Modern Age
How The Bible in Nature Provides an Antidote to Doubt and Despair

by

W. Kent Smith

in association with

Staten House

Books by W. Kent Smith

Lies My Professor Told Me About American Politics: Questions Concerning the Original Vision of the Founding Fathers

Conquering Cynicism in a Modern Age: How The Bible in Nature Provides an Antidote to Doubt and Despair

On Earth as It is On Heaven: The Promise of America, Technology, and the New Earth, Book One: The Promise of America

The Book of Days: In Search of the 5,500-year Prophecy Given to Adam About the Coming of Christ

The Book of Tales: Stories That Confirm the 5,500-year Prophecy Given to Adam About the Coming of Christ

Fish Tales (From the Belly of the Whale): Fifty of the Greatest Misconceptions Ever Blamed on The Bible, Reel One, The Hook #50-34

Fish Tales (From the Belly of the Whale): Fifty of the Greatest Misconceptions Ever Blamed on The Bible, Reel Two, The Line #33-18

Fish Tales (From the Belly of the Whale): Fifty of the Greatest Misconceptions Ever Blamed on The Bible, Reel Three, The Sinker #17-1

Fish Tales (From the Belly of the Whale): Fifty of the Greatest Misconceptions Ever Blamed on The Bible, The Complete Edition, Hook, Line, and Sinker #50-1

Tales of Forever: The Unfolding Drama of God's Hidden Hand in History, Book One: The Analyses – Part One

Tales of Forever: The Unfolding Drama of God's Hidden Hand in History, Book Two: The Tales – Part One

Tales of Forever: The Unfolding Drama of God's Hidden Hand in History, Book Three: The Tales – Part Two

Tales of Forever: The Unfolding Drama of God's Hidden Hand in History, Book Four: The Analyses – Part Two

Tales of Forever: The Unfolding Drama of God's Hidden Hand in History, The Complete Edition

For Scott, Dennis & David:

My comrades-in-arms and favorite cynics

Contents

A Prelude
The Quest for an Antidote
(Because False Hope is So Easy to Embrace and Real Hope is So Hard to Come By)..1

Chapter One
The Seeds of Cynicism
(Because Life is Full of Disappointments)...........................5

Chapter Two
The Joy of Cynicism
(Because Doubt Comes So Easily to the Human Race)......9

Chapter Three
The Paradox of Cynicism
(Because One Person's Doubt is Another Person's Certainty)...15

Chapter Four
Between Certainty and Doubt
(Because Free Will Can't Seem to Make Up its Mind)...31

Chapter Five
A Tale of Two Worlds
(Because Only Through the Fall Could We Know What It Means to Be Truly Human)..47

CHAPTER SIX
A Lack of Perspective
(Because Every Story in The Bible Needs to Be Told in Its Proper Context)..........60

CHAPTER SEVEN
A Recipe for Cynicism
(Because Dreams and Reality Rarely Coincide in the Way We Expect Them To)..........74

CHAPTER EIGHT
The Silence of God
(Because the Voice of Creation Speaks as Loudly as Any Biblical Book Ever Written)..........84

CHAPTER NINE
The Economy of Nature
(Because God Always Knew How to Transcend the Power of Death)..........103

CHAPTER TEN
From Economy to Ecology
(Because Death is the Only Means to the Renewal of Life)..........122

CHAPTER ELEVEN
The Death of Beauty
(Because Real Hope isn't Something You Keep in Your Pocket Like a Lucky Rabbit's Foot)..........142

BIBLIOGRAPHY..........165

ABOUT THE AUTHOR..........168

A Prelude

The Quest for an Antidote

(Because False Hope is So Easy to Embrace and Real Hope is So Hard to Come By)

> **TRUTH,** a noun
> "An ingenious compound of desirability and appearance. Discovery of truth is the sole purpose of philosophy, which is the most ancient occupation of the human mind and has a fair prospect of existing with increasing activity to the end of time."
>
> The Cynic's Word Book, Ambrose Bierce

AT ITS MOST basic level, the kind of cynicism we'll be speaking of here concerns the age-old tendency where it's so easy to view things like God or truth or justice as the stuff that only fools or con artists profess to believe in. In contrast to the simplicity of doubt and skepticism, there is the incredible difficulty of negotiating real faith or real hope.

The reasons for such cynicism are varied and complex, but essentially—and this is the main thrust of this work—it isn't because people outright reject or deny the existence of God or truth or justice, as one might assume. Instead, the main reason for cynicism is due to an overwhelming belief in God or truth or justice. Unfortunately, though, because that belief in the reality of such things is so often disappointed due to the presence of evil in the world, the inevitable response is despair that in turn creates the perfect recipe for cynicism. What's worse, the great irony of modern life is—in the wake of Western progress, democracy, and technology—the greater the level of our hope, the deeper is the level of our cynicism.

That said, *Conquering Cynicism in a Modern Age* traces the history of humanity's attitude toward God and the world, marred as it is by the presence of evil, particularly in terms of what is communicated in *The Bible*. That's because although cynicism, as a by-product of hope disappointed, has reached epidemic levels in today's world, it is by no means strictly a modern condition. In fact, it's as old as the most ancient dramas depicted in Scripture. As a result, what begins as a straightforward discussion of conquering cynicism in a modern world soon takes an unexpected turn as we journey forward through time, age after age, in a quest for an antidote to the most corrosive force in God's creation.

In the process of that search, we find ourselves surveying familiar territory, although it's territory that takes on new meaning in this ages-long quest. In this case, I'm talking about the ever-present role of the natural world, to uniquely communicate God's message to a humanity that is generally oblivious to what is right in front of them—a message of hope that is quite literally hidden in plain sight. This idea is most succinctly stated in Scripture, when the Apostle Paul described it this way:

> For what may be known about God is evident to all, because God has made it plain to them. For since the creation of the world, God's invisible qualities, His eternal power and divine nature have been clearly

seen, being understood from His workmanship so that mankind is without excuse.

The Book of Romans

As such, this message conveyed through the natural world around us, speaks just as loudly to those who don't believe in the God of *The Bible* as it does to those who do. More importantly—and this is the unexpected turn I alluded to earlier—our investigation into the natural world will reveal a startling twist. Because in examining the history of humanity's relationship to God's creation, we confront many facts that no typical science lesson ever imparts.

That's because, as it turns out, one of the most cynical theories of human existence, namely "evolution," could never have been formulated by Charles Darwin had he not inherited a school of thought that was utterly alien to his own atheistic perspective. That school of thought—developed by Christian natural philosophers beginning in the seventeenth century—described the intricate relationship between the Earth and all living things as a direct function of the God of *The Bible*. In time, each building upon the work of others, proponents of this new worldview were able to demonstrate how every aspect of the natural world exhibits consistent patterns, in spite of all its apparent randomness, which to the untrained eye gives the impression that Nature is simply the by-product of a disinterested Universe.

It was this unique worldview, then, bequeathed to us by men like Robert Boyle, John Ray, Kenelm Digby, Thomas Burnet, and Carl Linnaeus, that laid the foundation for many of our modern-day sciences, such as chemistry, biology, botany, zoology, anthropology, and ecology. This divinely-inspired worldview—this Economy of Nature, as it was called by both sacred and secular scholars in their quest to map out the observable qualities of our world—is what I'll demonstrate provides us with the antidote to what ails us most.

In short, what follows here is my attempt to restore a universal message imparted via God's creation so that not only will you learn how this worldview was hijacked and reworked to our subsequent hurt, but you will also come to understand the original purpose that the greatest minds of natural philosophy intended for their discovery. In doing so, you will encounter a most unexpected remedy to one of the most destructive forces in God's creation—more corrosive than sin and the enemy of hope—yet one that can be conquered by even a child ... the power of cynicism.

CHAPTER ONE
The Seeds of Cynicism
(Because Life is Full of Disappointments)

> **EXISTENCE,** *a noun*
> "A transient, horrible, fantastic dream."
> *The Cynic's Word Book,* Ambrose Bierce

STYLES COME, and styles go, but what never goes out of style is cynicism. When adversity strikes, do we embrace the challenge with dignity and grace? Do we rise to the occasion with steely resolve? Or do we instead criticize other people, the Universe, or God for ganging up on us? And why not? We're only human, right? And if you're human, then your life is full of disappointments; and wherever there are disappointments, Lord knows, cynicism is sure to follow.

Now understand, when I say cynicism, I'm not talking about its cousins—skepticism, pessimism, and nihilism. By definition, a skeptic doubts the authenticity of certain ideas that claim to be true, which still opens the door for a change of heart should evidence convince them otherwise. A pessimist sees the worst in everything, and goes through life without much hope, yet this still doesn't rule out that they'll make more calculated decisions, thus increasing the possibility for success in life. And the nihilist believes that life has no meaning or purpose, and so rejects such concepts as truth and morality. However, this personal sense of uncertainty and powerlessness doesn't always lead to total negativity as one might expect but can motivate a person toward unexpected avenues of renewal and growth.

Cynicism, by contrast, turns out to contain the seeds of a much more toxic sort than any of its cousins. That's because while skepticism, pessimism, and nihilism target abstractions such as ideas, values, and morals, the cynic's favorite targets are people, and more specifically, what motivates people. When certain ones wax on about faith, hope, and love, the cynic instantly mocks them because in their view buying into such nonsense demonstrates how uneducated, unsophisticated, and unrealistic they really are.

Take, for example, the view of one of America's foremost cynics, the nineteenth-century writer, journalist, and satirist Ambrose Bierce. When Bierce defined the cynic as "a blackguard whose faulty vision sees things as they are, not as they ought to be," he seems to take great pride in his self-styled role of watching out for the "less sophisticated." From the cynic's intellectual high ground, the things many of us cling to, such as a belief in justice or destiny, are so obviously shams that those who hold such views are deemed self-serving, manipulative liars, or worse, willing dupes who need to be protected. Ironically, though, while cynics offer their advice with such an air of concern for those they see as needing their help, there is also a distinct undercurrent to their remarks that makes it clear the cynic believes those who fail to heed their warnings deserve to be deceived.

On the subject of "justice," Bierce called it "a commodity which in a more or less adulterated condition the State sells to the citizen as a reward for his allegiance, taxes and personal service." And concerning "destiny," Bierce observed it was "a tyrant's authority for crime and a fool's excuse for failure." Notice how in both cases Bierce's target wasn't the idea itself but, rather, the ones with wrong motives who endorsed such foolishness. In Bierce's worldview, then, the victims are no less guilty than the villains, because only tyrants and fools peddle concepts like "destiny," both to their own hurt. Likewise, only the State and its citizens, who are both subject to corruptibility, buy into the fallacy that something as arbitrary as "justice" can actually be had ... for a price, that is.

As such, no one is beyond the scorn of the cynical mind, not even God. In fact, the God of *The Bible* is considered an even worthier target for the cynic's contempt and ridicule, since He's thought to be the One to blame for all of humanity's problems. Whether it's because He's too callous, too barbaric, or too inept—you name it—He's presumed guilty as charged. He is, after all, the One Who is responsible for unleashing evil upon the world, isn't He?

Not only that, but the cynic also adheres to an even more peculiar train of thought: If anyone fails to live up to the high calling of God, cynics don't blame the people who fail to do so. No, it's not those who commit acts of greed, or abuse, or betrayal, or lust, or lying, or gluttony, or laziness, or theft, or adultery, or perversion, or murder, who are seen as being guilty of sin—no, no, no, certainly not. The real culprit, declares the cynic, is God Himself. As Bierce described it, with his signature acid wit:

> By what right, then, do royal rulers rule?
>   Whose is the sanction of their state and pow'r?
> He surely were as stubborn as a mule,
>   Who, God unwilling, could maintain an hour.
>
> His uninvited session on the throne, or air,
>   His pride securely in the presidential chair.

> Whatever is, is so by right divine;
>   Whate'er occurs, God wills it so. Good land!
> It were a wondrous thing if His design,
>   A fool could baffle, or a rogue withstand!
>
> If so, then God, I say (intending no offence)
>   Is guilty of contributory negligence.
>
>   *The Cynic's Word Book*

Never mind that it makes no sense based on any form of logic that I'm aware of, yet there it is—century upon century, verdict upon verdict, guilt upon guilt. God is blamed for crimes He never committed, while the real culprits are judged as though they were the victims in every case.

As to why cynics the world over, proudly and defiantly, cling to such a contrary view is the primary question, among others, that we'll focus on in the following work, *Conquering Cynicism in a Modern Age: How The Bible in Nature Provides an Antidote to Doubt and Despair.*

CHAPTER TWO

The Joy of Cynicism
(Because Doubt Comes So Easily to the Human Race)

> **DELUSION,** *a noun*
> "The father of a most respectable family, comprising Enthusiasm, Affection, Self-denial, Faith, Hope, Charity and many other goodly sons and daughters."
>
> *The Cynic's Word Book,* Ambrose Bierce

THE STORY presented in *The Bible* isn't one that describes a perfect world or a perfect people. And because it doesn't, it's argued that neither the human race nor the world were created by a perfect God. According to critics of *The Bible*, the presence of suffering, disease, and death in this imperfect world are undeniable proofs of their various claims regarding belief—or in their case, unbelief—in God. Either God doesn't exist at all, or if a Supreme Being does exist, he clearly isn't in control of the Universe and so is incapable of fixing what's happening on Earth. Or perhaps, he's just too busy with more important matters than that of caring for an unworthy species; or worst of all, he no longer gives a damn about us and has left us to our own devices from here on out.

However, in response to such lines of thought, I'd suggest an alternative interpretation of said proofs. I'd suggest, in light of the scriptural evidence in *The Book of Genesis*, that suffering, disease, and death are actually to be viewed in such a way as to flip the traditional script of the critics. And after reviewing said evidence in the following work, one might not only view suffering, disease, and death in a brand-new way but also the idea that God has been dethroned because the world isn't filled with perfect little darlings who live up to the notion that we're made in His image.

Admittedly, such a task isn't an easy one. It will take a great deal of examining the scriptural record that's available to us, as well as the human condition and the world as we know them today. That's because any genuine understanding of humanity's role on Earth as depicted in *The Bible* always requires tremendous effort, which is just another way of saying, the way of faith is hard—"real faith," that is, not pseudo-faith, otherwise known as "blind faith." In contrast to this "hard faith," there is what I'd call "easy doubt," otherwise known as "blind skepticism."

Not that being skeptical about some things is always bad, but in comparison to real faith, skepticism can easily become like a bad habit that one doesn't realize has suddenly become the norm. What began as a healthy critique of ultimate reality, in the face of so many abuses and misconceptions, soon turns into "easy skepticism," and before you know it, skepticism has metastasized into that more malignant form of doubt known as "cynicism." And once that happens, there's virtually no known cure to the mindset of the "hardcore cynic."

When it comes to such issues, then, of believing or doubting the claims of *The Bible*, it's typically analyzed in terms of a person's faith or lack thereof. As such, it's said that if you have faith, you're able to believe the message of Scripture; if you lack faith, then you can't help but doubt that message. But upon further analysis, this seems to me to be a gross oversimplification. That's because by narrowing the issue of belief in *The Bible* to a faith versus non-faith dichotomy, we're actually no closer to understanding why some people believe in Scripture and others don't. And by oversimplifying this issue, we're nowhere nearer to understanding how a perfect God can co-exist with imperfect humans inhabiting an imperfect world.

FOR AS LONG as I can remember, the question of whether or not we can trust the God of *The Bible* has come down to one's acceptance of the message of Scripture. When non-believers—variously called agnostics, atheists, and infidels—reject the biblical message, believers respond by presenting every kind of evidence they consider valid, both from Scripture and from Nature. In response, the hearers are said to determine their levels of faith or non-faith based on their response.

To prove this point, believers may point to the famous parable of Jesus and the "sower of the seed," where four types of "soil"—or mindsets, actually—were revealed by the degree to which each group received the teaching of Scripture. While three-quarters of the listeners were impervious to the message, one-quarter responded favorably. Naturally, the typical assumption has been that those who believed did so because they had faith, while the others did not.

But if that's the case, then I'm very curious to know: What, exactly, does that mean? To me, it's not enough to spout the glib verdict that "you just gotta have faith" to receive the biblical message. If, as we're told, it's the same message being expressed to each and every listener, what is it about the listener that creates this attitude of unbelief? Of course, many would claim it was due to the spiritual condition of the listeners themselves. Of course, they were sinners, it would be suggested; that's why they didn't have faith. The only problem with that train of thought is, if you believe the message of Scripture, then you're supposed to be on board with the overall message of the book, which states that all humans have sinned and fallen short of the glory of God. As such, then, we're all sinners by nature. And if that's true, then even those in the parable described as being "good soil" are just as likely to reject the message as those who constituted "bad soil."

That said, the mystery of why some people "have faith" but others "lack faith" doesn't seem to have anything to do with their so-called "spiritual state." What else could it be, then?

MANY YEARS ago, I heard a story about what was described as the "joy of agnosticism," in which it was said that agnosticism was a far easier philosophy of life to embrace than theism. While theism is defined as the belief in God as the creator of the Universe, intervening in it and sustaining a personal relation to His creatures, agnosticism states that nothing can be known of God's existence or of anything beyond material phenomena.

In contrast to the atheist, who flat out denies the existence of God, the agnostic claims neither belief nor disbelief in God. In either case, whether one embraces agnosticism or atheism, both are said to question any and all evidence offered by theism as proof of God's existence. In short, both the agnostic and the atheist find it easier to embrace doubt in contrast to the theist who struggle to embrace faith.

At this juncture, one needs to understand something very important. When I talk about such things as faith and doubt, it's easy to get lost in the traditional meanings of these words. And if this continues unchecked, then there's really no point in examining this question of why some people have faith and others don't. That's because when most people talk about faith, it's generally assumed that we're talking about "blind faith" as opposed to a faith that involves an experience-based analysis. It's assumptions like this that had Bierce railing against the traditional view of faith, when he described it as "belief without evidence in what is told by one who speaks without knowledge, of things without parallel." And because of this, most in turn can't help but buy into the misconception that people who do believe in the evidence of Scripture or Nature are naïve, gullible, or foolish for doing so.

As such, it's important to understand that throughout this work, I'm never talking about "blind faith." What I am talking about is best described as "hard faith," which is to say, faith that requires great effort and investigation to attain; and because of this it is equally important to understand that "hard faith" is never as cut-and-dry as even the most ardent believer would like it to be. Instead, because real faith is so difficult to achieve, it is always at best a tug of war between doubt and faith, between doubt and certainty. When considering this spiritual tug of war, I'm always reminded of two views expressed by two famous thinkers. On one hand, there is the eighteenth-century French philosopher Voltaire who said, "Doubt is not a pleasant condition, but certainty is absurd." And on the other hand, there is the nineteenth-century English philosopher John Stuart Mill who said, "There is no such thing as absolute certainty, but there is assurance sufficient for the purposes of human life."

And herein lies the crucial difference between agnosticism and theism, because doubt comes so easily to the human race, while certainty comes so hard. That's why when I talk about such things as agnosticism, skepticism, and cynicism, I can talk about them in terms of the "joy" they bring. While the agnostic sits in his or her ivory tower and belittles anyone they deem foolish enough to embrace the message of *The Bible*, the theist wrestles daily with the same evidence that confronts the agnostic. But instead of casually, joyfully, dismissing it like the agnostic, the theist anxiously, painstakingly, attempts to reconcile said evidence.

As such, these two worldviews spawn two very different personality types. The ever-seeking believer sees himself or herself as a creature subject to the divine will and though plagued with an inevitable sense of guilt and uncertainty never loses sight of their ultimate destiny beyond one's mortal self. Compare that to the happy-go-lucky agnostic who thinks himself or herself above all the nonsense, all the hypocrisy, all the self-deception of their less sophisticated counterparts who they see as wallowing in so much self-pity and self-recrimination.

As the Scriptures describe it, there are the troubled ones who constantly struggle to make sense of the incongruities of life, and who groan: "Woe is me, I'm undone. Please God, be merciful to me—a sinner." Then there are the others who live contentedly, high above all the head games played by those whom they view as religious zealots, and who exclaim: "Joy is me, I'm immune. Please folks, be sensible with me—a realist."

CHAPTER THREE

The Paradox of Cynicism

(Because One Person's Doubt is Another Person's Certainty)

> **RELIGION,** *a noun*
> "A daughter of Hope and Fear, explaining to Ignorance the nature of the Unknowable."
>
> *The Cynic's Word Book,* Ambrose Bierce

AS WITH ALL noble human endeavors—arts, sciences, philosophy, exploration, and the like—this work strives to fulfill a higher purpose. As alluded to at the start, I'm endeavoring to reconcile the paradox of the human condition as set forth in *The Bible*. In short, I'm looking to answer the question: How can imperfect people, living in an imperfect world, co-exist with a perfect God? And just as importantly, I'm hoping to answer this question without succumbing to that age-old condition so endemic to the human race: cynicism.

Keep in mind, though, in my attempt, I'm all too aware of a potential irony: Even if I succeed in this noble endeavor—in my view at least—the end result may still never have the desired effect when seen through the lens of cynicism.

To understand why, we first need to consider how cynicism impacts the human condition:

Cynicism is an attitude characterized by a general distrust of the motives of others. A cynic has a lack of faith or hope in people whom they see as being motivated by ambition, desire, greed, gratification, materialism, goals, and opinions that the cynic perceives as vain, unobtainable, or ultimately meaningless.

The term originally derives from the ancient Greek philosophers, the Cynics, who rejected conventional goals of wealth, power, and honor. They practiced shameless nonconformity with social norms in religion, manners, housing, dress, or decency, instead advocating the pursuit of virtue in accordance with a simple and natural way of life.

Wikipedia

According to tradition, one of the founding members of this cynical movement was Diogenes of Sinope, born in ancient Greece around 410 B.C. Although none of his writings have survived, much of what he said was recorded by others, among them, Plutarch and Philo.

The term *cynic* derives from the ancient Greek *kynikos*, meaning "dog" or "dog-like." Calling them this was intended as an insult for their blatant rejection of convention and willingness to live on the streets, but Diogenes actually reveled in the title, stating that "other dogs bite their enemies, but I bite my friends to save them." He was also heard to say, "I am Diogenes the Dog. I nuzzle the kind, bark at the greedy, and bite scoundrels." When people laughed at him because he walked backward beneath the portico, he said to them, "Aren't you ashamed that you walk backward along the whole path of existence, yet you blame me for walking backward along the path of the promenade?" Once Diogenes saw the officials of a temple leading away someone who had stolen a bowl belonging to the treasurers, and he said, "The great thieves are leading away the little thief." When seized and dragged off to King Philip of Macedonia, he was asked who he was, to which he replied, "A spy upon your insatiable greed."

Speaking of the original cynic, the ancient Greek philosopher Dio Chrysostom wrote:

> Diogenes was surprised by the fact that had he claimed to be a physician for the teeth, everybody would flock to him who needed to have a tooth pulled; yes, and by heavens, had he professed to treat the eyes, all who were suffering from sore eyes would present themselves, and similarly, if he had claimed to know of a medicine for diseases of the spleen or for gout or for running of the nose.
>
> But when he declared that all who should follow his treatment would be relieved of folly, wickedness, and intemperance, not a man would listen to him or seek to be cured by him ... as though it were worse for a man to suffer from an enlarged spleen or a decayed tooth than from a soul that is foolish, ignorant, cowardly, rash, pleasure-loving, illiberal, irascible, unkind, wicked and, in fact, utterly corrupt.
>
> *On Virtue, or Diogenes*

Ironically, when one examines the roots of cynicism, it should escape no one who has ever studied the teachings of Jesus of Nazareth that these ancient Cynics were actually successors of the Hebrew prophets as well as forerunners of Christ Himself.

After all, who more than the Hebrew prophets were characterized by their outcry against ambition, greed, and materialism? Who railed more against conventional goals of wealth, power, and honor? Who more than Jesus conformed less with the social norms of His day, in religion and manners?

As to the parallels between this original form of cynicism and the teachings of Christ, Dio Chrysostom further recorded, in the century immediately following the birth of Christianity:

> Just as the good physician should go and offer his services where the sick are most numerous, so, said Diogenes, the man of wisdom should take up his abode where fools are thickest in order to convict them of their folly and reprove them.
>
> *On Virtue, or Diogenes*

However, while the cynics of old and their modern-day counterparts are characterized by a general lack of faith or hope as a result of their view of human motives, Jesus and His disciples never succumbed to the negativity that is associated with full-blown cases of cynicism.

Like all things pertaining to the human condition, then, what is valuable in moderation is dangerous when excessively indulged in. In fact, it's this paradoxical quality of cynicism that lies at the heart of the human dilemma. That's why I'm suggesting in the following work that we differentiate between the healthy and malignant aspects of this thing called cynicism. So, in the interest of steering clear of any negative aspects associated with cynicism, I'd suggest that when *The Bible* describes how the prophets and Jesus address the human condition, they're not so much being "cynical" as they're being "suspicious."

BEFORE THE Greek cynics arrived on the scene, warning us about foolishness, ignorance, and cowardice, the Hebrew prophet Jeremiah found himself in a situation that prefigured the dilemma of Diogenes of Sinope. It's said of Diogenes that one day he was seen wandering about the city in broad daylight yet he was carrying a lit lantern. When asked what he was doing, he replied, "I'm looking for an honest man." According to Joshua J. Mark:

> This was his way of exposing the hypocrisy and sham of polite societal conventions. By holding a literal light up to people's faces in broad daylight, Diogenes forced them to recognize their participation in practices that prevented them from living truthfully.
>
> *World History Encyclopedia 2014*

In the case of Jeremiah, he'd been tasked with communicating God's anger toward the southern kingdom of Judah who was on the verge of divine judgment for their persistent rebellion against the Lord. In essence, Jeremiah was the voice of divine suspicion. Said God to His mouthpiece:

> "Go up and down the streets of Jerusalem, look around and consider, search through her squares. If you can find just one person who deals honestly and seeks the truth, I'll forgive this city. Although they say, 'As surely as the Lord lives,' they still swear falsely…"
>
> So Jeremiah said, "Lord, don't Your eyes look for truth? You struck them, but they felt no pain; you crushed them, but they refused correction. They made their faces harder than stone and refused to repent. I thought, 'These are only the poor; they're foolish, for they don't know the way of the Lord, the requirements of their God. So I'll go to the leaders and speak to them; surely they know the way of the Lord, the requirements of their God.'"
>
> But with one accord they had all broken off the yoke and torn off the bonds. And the Lord said, "The

people of Judah have been utterly unfaithful to Me. They lied about Me when they said, 'The Lord won't do anything! No harm will come to us; we'll never see sword or famine.' But the prophets of Judah are but wind, and My word of truth isn't in them; so let what they say be done to them."

The Book of Jeremiah

Several key takeaways present themselves here that will prove important throughout this work. First, the God of *The Bible*, from age to age, encourages—no, commands, actually—that we be suspicious of those who pretend to be *outwardly* what they are not *inwardly*. Second, any attempts to get away with this kind of subterfuge will be searched out and tested by God and His various agents, such as prophets, seers, poets, and the like, as well as by circumstances, historically, naturally, supernaturally. And third, God's typical vehicle of judgment will be to mirror the very words of rebellious people so that their own profession announces their subsequent punishment.

NOW IN USING this word "suspicious," keep in mind the context in which I'm using it. I'm not talking about the same thing that applies to cynicism, in that cynicism is defined as a "general" lack of faith in the motives of others. By definition, suspicion is "the act of suspecting something is wrong without proof or evidence." The difference between being cynical and being suspicious, then, is that the suspicious mind can be altered by the introduction of tangible proof or evidence, while the cynical mind is impervious to it. As such, evidence is capable of shifting one's perspective from that of suspicion to that of conviction, as to either innocence or guilt in the case of a legal matter, or belief or disbelief in the case of an intellectual matter. By contrast, the cynical mind taints one's perspective in regard to all such evidence, in effect altering the very thing that could sway someone's perspective had they not been so inclined toward a cynical view of life.

Dick Keyes poignantly illustrates this, in his book *Seeing Through Cynicism*, in the Pharisees' reaction to the miraculous events surrounding Jesus' raising of Lazarus from the dead. Upon Lazarus emerging from his tomb, at just a word from Jesus, the onlookers were all confronted with the same evidence. But did they all react the same way to the evidence?

Imagine, if you will, what you'd have been thinking during those long, drawn-out moments after Jesus uttered the command: "Lazarus, come forth!" No doubt if any of us were there at the time, we'd all rightly have been just as suspicious as anyone else standing there in anticipation. What's more, we'd have been suspicious because Jesus Himself warned us to be wary of false prophets who claim to speak for God but do not. Based on that, then, who would've blamed anyone for doubting that anyone would be emerging from the tomb that day.

But when Lazarus did walk out, alive and well, how did the people react then? Was everyone there equally convinced that Jesus was the Son of God? Were all of their suspicions suddenly displaced by belief? Did they all put away their doubts and accept that they were eyewitnesses to God's power and presence in their midst?

As Keyes described the reaction of the crowd, he drew a sharp distinction between those who were moved to believe in Jesus' divine status that day and the Jewish religious leaders who simply couldn't see things the same way. Speaking of those leaders, he said:

> The evidential force of what they had just seen was lost on them, eclipsed by their overwhelming anxiety. So they called a special council and concluded,

"If we let Jesus go on like this, everyone will believe in him, and the Romans will come and destroy both our holy place and our nation."

So, they immediately began plans to kill Jesus ... and Lazarus also, "since it was on account of him that many Jews were deserting and were believing in Jesus."

What was the problem here? Was raising a man who was dead for four days not enough evidence to convince them that Jesus was the Son of God? In one sense the problem was the reverse. There was too much evidence... What they saw in Jesus was not a revealer of God but only a threat to their power and security.

Seeing Through Cynicism: A Reconsideration of the Power of Suspicion

AS FOR GOD'S inevitable efforts in searching out and testing His people's disobedience, we see a similar dynamic at work in the case of Jeremiah and the Judahites in his day. God easily saw through the surface behavior of the people in their stubborn posturing; although they declared, "As surely as the Lord lives," their rebellious behavior betrayed their real attitude. As usual, God's suspicions weren't lacking in proof or evidence, and more importantly, neither was that proof or evidence altered by any cynical view on God's part. Then compare that honest awareness with the dishonest reaction of the people in response to God's chastisement, which was actually designed to get His people's attention in order to steer them toward repentance. Instead of acknowledging the true nature of their predicament, they responded like spoiled children who, when spanked, mockingly moan, "Oh, wow, that didn't even hurt."

Throughout the scriptural record depicting the history of God's people, we see this pattern repeating itself again and again. God calls a person or a group to fulfill a purpose on His behalf, but instead of maintaining a proper balance in that calling, they turn responsibility into privilege, and freedom into license. In doing so, they turn opportunity into failure, and hope into misery.

For example, Adam was commissioned to subdue the Earth and fill it with his children who were to serve the Lord throughout all generations. Instead, Adam succumbed to the wiles of the devil, then when given a chance to take responsibility for his actions, he blamed everyone but himself, saying, "The woman You gave me, Lord, ate first, then she gave me some, and I ate, too."

Here we have the first recorded occurrence of cynicism impacting the human condition. By going along with Eve in partaking of the Forbidden Fruit, Adam revealed his distrust of God's motives in the divine prohibition to avoid eating from the Tree of Knowledge. Consequently mankind, rather than ruling the Earth, became a slave to the elemental things of the Earth, and so mortality began to overtake the human race. Not only that, but the cynical mind was also handed the first dagger in the history of its pointing to God's supposed indifference toward suffering, disease, and death. And so, from that point onward, cynicism gave birth to cynicism upon cynicism.

Similarly, God called the sons of Jacob to carry on with the mission that He'd called Abraham and Isaac to fulfill: Be a light to the world and the salt of the Earth. In short, they were to bring the whole world to a knowledge of the God of Abraham, Isaac, and Jacob—to magnify the Lord in the midst of the nations of the Earth. And for a while, everything was proceeding quite nicely.

Among the many blessings that God had bestowed on Jacob's sons, en route to getting that job done: Judah was chosen to bring forth the kings of the clan, Levi was to provide spiritual guides, Benjamin would supply light bearers of wisdom, and Dan was the shipbuilder who would facilitate a series of seafaring migrations.

All was going nicely, that is, until Joseph began to share the strange dreams he was having with his brothers, and because these dreams seemed to indicate this young upstart—as his older, more illustrious brothers saw him—was planning a "take-over," his brothers grew so jealous they considered the unthinkable. Out of pure spite, the brothers sold Joseph to a caravan of Ishmaelites who took him to Egypt, and then they lied to their father by making Jacob think a wild animal had eaten him.

Just think: Like Adam before them, how might Joseph's brothers reacted had they simply trusted God to know what He was doing in calling them to their task? To me, their actions speak volumes, revealing a complete lack of awareness as to their place in the divine plan of the ages. Because had they truly been confident in God's choice, they'd never have succumbed to their jealousy of Joseph. Had they not reinterpreted their divinely-appointed roles in that plan, they would never have resorted to taking things into their own hands. In short, jealousy gave birth to cynicism, which by its very nature triggered a loss of faith in the motives of even their own flesh and blood, Joseph.

Not only that, but cynicism also ate at the root of their trust in God's motives whom they undoubtedly saw as inspiring this upstart's rebellion, considering the ancient attitude toward dreams. Were it not for Joseph receiving these dreams, only he would've been seen as the guilty party. But because Joseph was apparently being egged on via divine inspiration, the brothers couldn't help but see this as a betrayal of a higher order. So, when the brothers showed Joseph's torn and bloodied coat of many colors to their father, they were able to look him straight in the eye and, without flinching, lie to him about how "Joseph was killed by a wild animal," instead of breaking down and confessing to their crime as they might have under ordinary circumstances.

Now admittedly, if one were looking for the perfect scenario to prove the cynical view that a perfect God couldn't possibly be involved with this bunch, this is it. When honestly looking at events like this in *The Bible*, one can't help but hang one's head in disgust, to think that God would ever choose these scoundrels to represent Him. I mean, really, how could any of this provide light and salt to people who are seeking to know God?

But here is where I'd begin to ask: What, exactly, does Scripture mean when it says that God intends the offspring of Israel to be light and salt? If that means these human offspring are to be light and salt, in and of themselves, then clearly cynics have absolute cause for their case. However, just as I earlier spoke of flipping the script about how we typically view suffering, disease, and death, I'd also like to introduce a new way to view how God intends biblical Israel to fulfill this mission of being light and salt.

While the brothers of Joseph obviously failed to live up to God's plan willingly, this has never meant that God's plan of the ages would fail because of human fallibility. That's because even though the tragedy of Joseph being sold into Egyptian bondage didn't exemplify light and salt from a human standpoint, it did set the stage for a much larger drama of which the brothers of Joseph could never have imagined they'd play a part.

AGAIN, THE timeless patterns of Scripture reveal a truth hidden to the cynical mind that is impervious to such evidence, while the merely suspicious mind is capable of being swayed if only it's willing to confront said evidence. Case in point, at first glance Joseph's debacle at the hands of his jealous brothers seems to confirm the age-old notion that if God does exist, He certainly doesn't care about human suffering. Certainly, when one looks through a cynical lens at the events depicted in *The Bible*, it's very easy to miss the "big picture," as it were.

But recall, if you will, the scene we described earlier involving Jeremiah and those rebellious Judahites whom God searched out as to their outward appearance while seeking to hide their inward reality. Outwardly, the people declared, "As the Lord lives," yet inwardly, according to God, they were swearing falsely. And in response, the verdict of God through the mouth of Jeremiah was, "So let what they say be done to them." What, exactly, did they say? They said, "The Lord won't do anything! No harm will come to us; we'll never see sword or famine." But because there was no truth in their words, the very words they uttered backfired on them and in fact formulated their own judgment in the form of the swords that the fearsome Babylonians brought against them and the famine that afterward overtook the land of Judah.

As for the words of Joseph's brothers that came back to haunt them, they are those which they spoke just prior to their dastardly deed. As the Scriptures describe it:

> Now Joseph's brothers saw him in the distance, and before he arrived, they plotted to kill him. "Here comes the dreamer!" they said to one another. "Come, let's kill him and throw him into a pit. We can say a vicious animal devoured him. Then we'll see what becomes of his dreams!"
>
> *The Book of Genesis*

Little did they know but one day they would come to know what became of his dreams, because as it turned out, Joseph's bondage in Egypt set the stage for the salvation of Jacob and his family, which foreshadowed the ultimate drama in *The Bible*, that of Jesus and His role in the salvation of all mankind, who were typified by Jacob's family.

As the story goes, once Joseph was delivered into the hands of the Egyptian official Potiphar, he became the unwitting participant in a series of events that elevated him to a position of great power. After interpreting Pharaoh's strange dreams, Joseph was awarded the position of viceroy of Egypt. Then famine in Palestine forced Jacob's sons down to Egypt in search of food, and without recognizing him, the brothers came face to face with Joseph as he sat on Egypt's throne. As it is written:

> Joseph was no longer able to control his feelings in front of his servants, so he ordered them all to leave the room. No one else was with him when Joseph told his brothers who he was.
>
> He cried with such loud sobs that the Egyptians heard it, and the news was taken to the king's palace.
>
> Joseph said to his brothers, "I'm Joseph. Is my father still alive?" But when his brothers heard this, they were so terrified that they couldn't answer him. Then Joseph said to them, "Please come closer."
>
> They did, and he said, "I am your brother Joseph, whom you sold into Egypt. Now don't be upset or blame yourselves because you sold me here. It was really God Who sent me ahead of you to save your lives.
>
> "This is only the second year of famine in the land; there will be five more years in which there will be neither plowing nor reaping. God sent me ahead of you to rescue you in this amazing way and to make sure that you and your children survive. So it wasn't really you who sent me here but God."
>
> *The Book of Genesis*

But what does the cynical mind see in the debacle of Joseph? Doubtlessly, it sees only what it's conditioned to see; it sees only failure with no hope of redemption whatsoever. It sees the same thing it sees in Adam's fall from grace, the same thing it sees in Judah's fall from grace. Essentially, the cynical mind falls victim to its own devices; and it does so by failing to remember what Bierce once observed:

> A cheap and easy cynicism rails at everything. The master of the art accomplishes the formidable task of discrimination.
>
> *A Cynic Looks at Life*

In other words, rather than see the story of Joseph's betrayal in the context of the entire narrative of *The Bible*, the cynical mind recalls only the events concerning the betrayal and so thinks itself justified in insisting there's no use serving a God Who allows such suffering and injustice. In short, it fails to discriminate between how Joseph's betrayal looks on a personal level, in terms of God's apparent failure to protect him, and how it looks on a national level, in terms of how it set the stage for a higher purpose on behalf of God's people in general.

In contrast to the limited view of the cynical mind, the merely suspicious mind sees more than meets the eye. Of course it grieves in response to the initial evidence that reveals the human tragedy for what it is. It, too, confronts the disappointment caused by the betrayal of Joseph's brothers, but unlike the cynical mind, it chooses not to reinterpret the story in terms of its own experience tainted as it may be by its own disappointments. Most importantly, it resists the urge to sugar-coat the events as though they weren't as bad as they first appeared, because to do so would be just as foolish as the cynical mind that refuses to be comforted by the evidence of God's providential hand that entered into said events to work out a much different ending than anyone might have anticipated.

In the final analysis, regarding such instances of injustice and suffering, we see just how the suspicious mind is capable of doing what the cynical mind can never do, which is to allow all the facts to weigh in on the final verdict as to God's motives in allowing certain tragic events to occur in the first place. This ability of the merely suspicious mind to remain elastic in the face of the many incongruities of life is clearly what sets it apart from the cynical mind and is what enables it to remain open to new evidence as it's introduced along the way.

Without this elasticity, it would also certainly succumb to the all-too-human tendency to chalk up Joseph's story as being just another example of a "happy ending" so common in fairy tales but not in real life. And really who can blame anyone for not ruling out the possibility that it was all too good to be true, just as no one can be blamed for thinking the same thing about Lazarus walking out of that tomb at just a word from Jesus. After all, *The Bible* is clearly less concerned about happy endings and more concerned about the question of what is true and what is false.

All things considered, then, how can we determine that something is true and not simply too good to be true? When are outward appearances covering up inward falsehoods? When is suspicion warranted in determining such matters? And when has a healthy suspicion ceased to be valid and thus metastasized into a malignant cynicism that has no redeeming value?

These are some of the questions addressed throughout this work, in the process of asking: How does cynicism affect our view of the most important issues that concern us as human beings? How does it affect our understanding of the world, ourselves, and others? How does it shape our attitude toward our most important institutions, values, and beliefs? And in a world yearning to know what is worthy of our trust, how do we adequately explain how a perfect God expects us to relate to suffering, disease, and death in an imperfect world?

CHAPTER FOUR

Between Certainty and Doubt

(Because Free Will Can't Seem to Make Up its Mind)

> **INCOMPOSSIBLE,** *an adjective*
> "Unable to exist if something else exists. Two things are incompossible when the world of being has scope enough for one of them, but not enough for both—as in Walt Whitman's poetry or God's mercy to man."
>
> *The Cynic's Word Book,* Ambrose Bierce

EVERY DAY, we're faced with a dizzying array of choices, most of which we resolve unconsciously rather than consciously. We do this either out of necessity or conditioning, but rarely do we consciously pause to consider choosing a different resolution along life's path. Among the factors that shape our decisions is our worldview, which is guided by our hopes and fears, our doubts and certainties, our expectations and disappointments. And among the various worldviews held by humans, the one we're most concerned with in this work is how our unique perspective of a Supreme Being inevitably shapes the world we live in.

Do you believe or disbelieve in a God? Do you believe that God is interested or disinterested in the lives of humans? Do you believe that God is capable or incapable of governing humanity in a perfect manner? Do you believe that God is so far above and beyond us that He can't relate to us on a personal level? Or do you believe that God can relate to us on a personal level despite His transcendence?

Then again, maybe, if you're like most humans, you'd admit that at various times throughout your life, you've maintained any or all of the previous worldviews. Again, whether you've done this consciously or unconsciously isn't the issue. What's important is, the God of *The Bible*—Who we're most concerned with here—understands all too well how this may be the case, and yet condemns no one for shifting from one perspective to another.

Now at this point I imagine that some folks who believe in *The Bible* might be thinking: Excuse me, where does it say that God doesn't condemn anyone for unbelief? Well, you have heard of Elijah, the prophet, haven't you? One minute he was bravely defying Jezebel and the priests of Baal, by miraculously calling down fire from Heaven, but no sooner had he pulled off the miracle of the century than he did a complete about-face:

> So Jezebel sent a messenger to Elijah, saying, "May the gods deal with me, and ever so severely, if by this time tomorrow I don't make your life like those you killed!" And Elijah was afraid and ran for his life. When he came to Beersheba in Judah, he left his servant there, while he himself traveled a day's journey into the wilderness. He sat down under a broom tree and prayed that he might die. "I've had enough, Lord," he said. "Take my life, for I'm no better than my fathers."
>
> *The First Book of Kings*

Now does that sound like the same guy who worked in concert with the Lord God of Israel in calling forth fire from Heaven?

Then there was Jonah, that other fairly famous prophet, who was actually hoping God would condemn the Ninevites to oblivion and was disappointed that He was willing to accept their repentance at face value.

> Jonah, however, was greatly displeased, and he became angry. So he prayed: "Lord, isn't this what I said while I was still in my own country? This is why I was so quick to flee toward Tarshish. I know You're a gracious and compassionate God, slow to anger, abounding in loving devotion—One who relents from sending disaster. And now, Lord, please take my life from me, for it's better for me to die than to live."
>
> *The Book of Jonah*

Talk about being suspicious beyond what was acceptable to God. Talk about doubting the motives of the very people to whom God had offered His grace. And this from the guy who famously survived three days and nights in the belly of a whale before he ever got a chance to preach to the Ninevites. But such is the peculiarities of faith and foolishness, even on the part of God's own messengers.

But wait, that's *The Old Testament*, you might say.

Well, how about Christ's disciples, Peter and Thomas? Don't you remember what happened with them? Peter was the first one among the disciples to recognize Jesus for Who He was, then he was the first to deny knowing Him in the hour of the Lord's crucifixion. As for Thomas, even after walking and talking with the Master Himself, he refused to believe that Christ rose from the dead until he personally touched the scars on His body. Wasn't it enough that they saw Jesus heal the sick and the blind and the deaf and the crippled? Didn't they witness Jesus walking on water with their own eyes? Yet when Christ urged them to keep the faith in their darkest hour, they failed miserably, and ever since, the names of Peter and Thomas have become synonymous with that of betrayal and doubt.

So correct me if I'm wrong, but aren't these perfect examples of individuals who bounced back and forth from one extreme to another, in terms of their belief or disbelief in God? Of course it is. This is, in fact, why these stories are in *The Bible*, to give hope to the hopeless, to encourage the fearful, to inspire the suspicious mind in us all, that maybe, just maybe, everything we've experienced concerning God in our lives isn't too good to be true. I mean, who are we to have the God of Israel, the Lord of Hosts, intervene in our lives? Have we lost our ever-loving minds, to think that God would really stoop to our puny level? Who are we kidding, anyway? But of course, this kind of healthy suspicion is perfectly valid. I mean if no one ever questioned the sheer improbability of having a real encounter with the Living God, they wouldn't be human, right?

The important thing to remember is: Where is the proper dividing line between a healthy suspicion, where we're urged to test our experience to make sure it's of God or not, and that other side of the coin, where the devil gleefully prods us into the realm of grim-faced cynicism? When do our doubts and fears push us headlong into questioning God's grace—something that we never really do deserve except as a function of a genuine faith connection? Because after all is said and done, experiencing the grace of God will still never change the fact that we're essentially caught between two worlds until the day we die.

That's because, based on the authority of Scripture itself, this world we live in—that of light and darkness, of good and evil, of certainty and doubt—is true to the nature of what God has created for us, as well as how God has created us to relate to this world.

Certainly the only thing more ironic than the dual nature of this world of ours is that in a most peculiar way the world is still somehow ours to shape depending on our worldview. Now, in saying this, I'm not at all suggesting that humans are in control of this world, as might be inferred by the biblical doctrine of Adam's original dominion of the creation. Clearly anyone who concedes to the biblical perspective must accept that we're now members of a fallen race living in a fallen world that bears both the beauty and grandeur of its original creation as well as the degradation and ugliness that has tarnished it. However, what I am saying is, as creatures of this God-ordained duality, the sons and daughters of Adam still possess a residual ability to determine how the world functions, for good or for ill. Think I'm making outlandish statements to this effect? What? Haven't you ever heard what the Scriptures describe:

> During the fourth watch of the night, Jesus went out to them, walking on the sea. When the disciples saw Him walking on water, they were terrified. "It's a ghost!" they said and cried out in fear.
> But Jesus spoke up at once: "Take courage! It's just Me. Don't be afraid."
> "Lord, if it is You," Peter replied, "command me to come to You on the water."
> "Come," said Jesus.
> Then Peter got down out of the boat, walked on the water, and came toward Jesus. But when Peter saw the strength of the wind, he was afraid, and beginning to sink, he cried out, "Lord, save me!"
> Immediately Jesus reached out His hand and took hold of Peter. "You of little faith," He said, "why did you doubt?"

And when they had climbed back into the boat, the wind died down. Then those who were in the boat worshiped Him, saying, "Truly, You are the Son of God!"

The Gospel of Matthew

Now, almost everyone has heard the story of Jesus walking on water—believers and unbelievers alike. But how many are familiar with the fact that *The Bible* records Peter walking on water, too? Here we have a perfect example for our purposes on several levels. First, we have a story that even the most ardent of Christians might be skeptical about. Second, because it's so shrouded in suspicion that the event is rarely the subject of sermons or commentaries. And third, there's no better scene to illustrate the idea that a peculiar trait resides in the human race which determines the very nature of the world we live in.

To what extent does your reaction to this scene reveal your own tendency toward cynicism? Are you as familiar with Peter's role in the story as you are with that of Jesus walking on water? And finally, how obvious is it to you why Peter stayed afloat and why he sank? For what it's worth let me provide my thinking about the dynamics of this scene, in the context of this work, because it certainly seems logical to me that as long as Peter remained focused on Jesus alone, his divinely inspired adventure outside the boat held firm and steady. But upon turning his gaze to the wind and the waves, Peter was suddenly reduced to his fallen, mortal self, and he began to sink like a stone.

Naturally, one's verdict in the matter hinges on two things. Are you cynical to the point of disbelief? Or are you merely suspicious about belief in such an impossible event? Remember the criterion for such divergent attitudes? One is impervious to further evidence that might support the possibility, while the other can be persuaded when confronted by corroborating evidence. In this case, I'd submit evidence in the form of scriptural testimony offered by Jesus Himself:

> To the Roman centurion, Jesus said, "As you've believed, so it will be done to you…"
>
> To the blind man, He said, "According to your faith, it will be done…"
>
> And to the Canaanite woman, He said, "Woman, your faith is great; it will be done for you as you desire."
>
> *The Gospel of Matthew*

In each of the preceding cases, the faith of an individual was the catalyst for a miracle of someone's physical transformation. The Roman centurion's servant was healed, the blind man had his sight restored, and the Canaanite woman's daughter was similarly healed.

But all this wasn't new with the coming of Christ. As the incarnate word of God, Jesus was just speaking forth the mind of God from the beginning, as the writer of *Proverbs* said:

> The words of a man's mouth are as deep waters, and the wellspring of wisdom as a flowing brook…
>
> A fool's mouth is his destruction, and his lips are the snare of his soul…
>
> A man's belly shall be satisfied with the fruit of his mouth, and with the increase of his lips shall he be filled. Death and life are in the power of the tongue, and those who love it will eat its fruit.
>
> *The Book of Proverbs*

So you see, there really does seem to be scriptural evidence for the fact that, while we're undoubtedly fallen beings forever altered by God's decree upon Adam, we still inherently possess a peculiar power to shape the world we live in according to either our certainty or our doubt.

IN THE STRUGGLE between certainty and doubt, many factors weigh into the fray. On one hand, there are those obvious clues to the presence of God in the Universe, which can't help but elicit a faith in such a God: The splendor of a desert sunset, the glory of a star-filled night sky, the magnificence of a lush island paradise. There's the beauty displayed in the animal kingdom: The exotic design of the peacock's feathers, the breathtaking breach of the ocean's surface by the humpback whale, the majestic demeanor of a roaring African lion. There's the beauty in humanity: A wide-eyed infant held securely in a loving mother's arms, a giggling child as it reaches for a father's outstretched hand, a lover's lips on the tear-stained cheek of their beloved.

Unfortunately, though, there's more to this life than the beauty that adorns the creation. There's also a tragic side to all that's good and wholesome in the Universe—a dark mirror, reflecting back a world of sadness and pain, of suffering and disease, of cruelty and death. Worse still, many point to this gross negativity in an attempt to undermine a faith in a God of such a topsy-turvy world. According to them, as long as suffering, disease, and death exist, we don't need any more proof concerning the utter futility in believing in a God Who would allow such horrors.

For unbelievers, this is one of the oldest arguments they offer in their attempt to undermine the idea of God's existence. In pointing to suffering, disease, and death, it's as though they've discovered some perverse flaw in God's creation that He's too embarrassed to admit He can't control and is therefore powerless to fix. For believers, this is one of the most painful aspects they face in their attempt to embrace the knowledge of God's existence. In confronting suffering, disease, and death, they often struggle with the nagging question of how these great enemies can exist in a world created by a loving God.

In confronting this double-edged dilemma, then, it's my hope to provide an answer, based on the available scriptural evidence, which will satisfy the demands of both parties. But before I do, let's first establish what we're looking for here, because the real problem, as I see it, isn't suffering, disease, and death *per se*. What we're talking about is suffering, disease, and death in the context of how they cause us to view God as being aloof by nature and therefore untouched by our predicament. In short, the problem these core issues speak to is the belief that even if God exists, based on our day-to-day experience, He just isn't as concerned with our pain and suffering as we'd like Him to be. The real problem, then, is the way that suffering, disease, and death undermine our view of God—to unbelievers, as proof of His non-existence; to believers, as an obstacle to faith in His promises.

So, if there's any truth to this logic, the question we'll look to answer when we turn to Scripture is: Does suffering, disease, and death negate God's faithfulness simply by virtue of their existence in our Universe?

In the process of investigating this question, though, I'd like to mention one more thing about God's aloofness—the one thing, actually, that anyone faces when dealing with this issue. When it comes to explaining this aloofness, it's quite common for theologians to point to God's holiness. God, they insist, is aloof because He's holy and we're not. Therefore, it's perfectly natural for God to distinguish Himself by being wholly separate from His admittedly sinful creation.

But in answer to such a view, I'd insist that, however holy that God is—of which Scripture is quite clear—there's still insufficient evidence to support the idea that His aloofness is entirely a function of His holiness. Yes, God is holy. Yes, His glory and perfection are without compare. Yes, His purity is above all and beyond all. But just because He is all of that, it still doesn't adequately explain the true nature of God's aloofness.

That's because any discussion of God's holiness as a basis for the separation between God and us rarely takes into account that, in addition to God's holiness, there is His love. In other words, if God were only perfect in terms of moral absoluteness, then we could understand why, due to an abhorrence of human imperfection, He'd distance Himself from us. But because God isn't just holy and righteous but also loving and merciful, He's perfectly free to relate to us, and be with us, as it were, without ever compromising that holiness and perfection.

Now certainly, there are those who might be tempted to accuse me of being presumptuous to insist on something like this. Certainly, many would argue the holiness of God is testified to in many ways throughout Scripture as being a barrier that separates God from humanity. Just look at all the symbolism, they'd argue, in the construction of the Tabernacle in the Wilderness, which, in turn, was incorporated in the construction of the Temple at Jerusalem. All this symbolically testified to the holiness of a God Who demanded nothing less than perfection before one could stand in His presence. And concerning this clear and obvious truth, I'd concur.

However, what also needs to be remembered is that none of what this symbolism reveals hindered Jesus from living amongst the common folk, even though none of them had yet to conform to the demands of a righteous God typified in what that sacred architecture meant to convey.

So, if Jesus were truly God in the flesh, as the Scriptures emphatically declare, then His holiness couldn't be diminished just because He was still in that flesh prior to

His crucifixion, resurrection, and ascension. If that were the case, then the fact that Jesus associated with His disciples as well as with tax collectors and prostitutes—without the demands of the Law being met through their ritual cleansing—tells us God's perfection can't account for His aloofness. Therefore, there must be some other reason for this aloofness.

THE FIRST THING we need to realize is, the presence of suffering, disease, and death in this world isn't the result of God's absence, or His indifference, or His aloofness; it's really the result of beings with free will who are exercising their free will. Because God prizes free will so much, He risked unleashing this unruly monster upon His Universe. First, He gave free will to Lucifer and the angels, which gave them the freedom to rebel and suffer the consequences of being expelled from Heaven. Then, He gave free will to Adam and Eve, which gave them the freedom to rebel and suffer the consequences of being expelled from the Garden of Eden.

And ever since these initial acts of free will, there began an inevitable chain reaction of freedom gone wrong that has in turn affected everything else God has done in human history. In response to the reckless actions of His own creation, then, God has literally been bound by His free will, to act in very specific ways, based on the promises He's made to humanity in the wake of their fall from grace. That's why we have *The Bible*, actually, to bear witness to this central fact of human existence, which is why it's referred to as a testament, that is, a contract, both old and new, hence *The Old Testament* and *The New Testament*.

So, when God made a contract with Adam and Eve, they weren't the only ones who were bound by that agreement. God was bound by it as well—for good and for bad. As a result, when Adam and Eve disobeyed God, they weren't the only ones who felt the sting of their disobedience. Their tragic fall from grace also affected God.

Now, this doesn't mean that God hasn't been able to establish new contracts with humanity, which is what He did with succeeding generations, all of which are clearly delineated throughout *The Bible*. He offered a new contract to Noah, then to Abraham, then to Moses, then to David. Then came an even better contract with Jesus, the Incarnate One, which was then ratified and codified through the work of the apostles, particularly through the teachings of Paul.

I say all this because what's lost, concerning the oft-repeated Scripture citing: "Jesus Christ is the same yesterday, today, and forever," is that God's actions toward us must always be assessed in light of the fact that it's not God Who changes. What changes are the contracts that God makes with humanity throughout history, which, by their very nature, bring about a change in the way He relates to us.

Thus, the original dilemma of both God and humanity is a direct consequence of Adam's disobedience, whereby God essentially found that He was—contractually speaking—an outsider of the very world He Himself had created. This doesn't mean He's an outsider in regard to His creation as a whole. It just means there's a kind of "residual effect," if you will, that the creation experiences because of Satan and Adam's original acts of disobedience. This residual effect can be seen in what scientists observe as the laws of nature, and what the apostles John and Paul described as the invisible power of God that upholds the order of the Universe, even while the human aspect of God's personality is submerged.

So, when it comes to the differences or similarities in God's behavior in *The Old Testament* versus *The New Testament*, we must always remember to view them through the prism of His contracts. Pay attention to God's contracts and our response to them, and we can't fail to detect a clear-cut pattern that sets the stage for a deeper understanding of why God does what He does.

WITH THAT IN mind, we turn next to the most important contract God has ever made with humanity, the one concerning life and death.

As anyone who's ever studied *The Bible* knows, God created Adam and Eve to be eternal from the beginning. Everywhere that the first couple looked—east, west, north, and south—the world was teeming with life. And although we have no idea how long they were in Eden—in terms of how we perceive time now—one thing is certain: From the moment they entered this world, they knew nothing but life. Yet ironically, even while in the midst of all that life, God's word warned Adam about something far different from what he'd ever known since his first moment on this planet.

> The Lord God took the man and placed him in the Garden of Eden to work it and to take care of it. And the Lord commanded the man: "You're free to eat from any tree in the garden, but you mustn't eat from the Tree of the Knowledge of Good and Evil, because in the day you do, you'll certainly die."
>
> *The Book of Genesis*

Try to imagine the scene, if you will. I know most of you have heard it described before, but try to imagine it in a way you've never considered until now. Try to imagine a world where every direction you looked, there was life … life … and *nothing but* life. Can you imagine what that would be like—to live in a world where there was no such thing as suffering, disease, or death? I know how difficult it is for me.

That's why I'd now like to flip the script, if I may, in an

attempt to make my point. Rather than imagining a world where we've never been, to see things the way Adam and Eve once did, try something else instead. Why am I asking this?

I'm doing it because all too often when we hear about this scene in which God is warning Adam about the consequences of his eating that Forbidden Fruit, we assume that we'd have done things differently had we been in that same position. So, to prove that none of us would've done any differently, imagine this: Rather than imagining Adam's world, where God strangely spoke of death, imagine our world—one that's the reverse of Adam's world—and imagine our reaction to God's promise of life. It's not too hard, after all, because in a stunning turn of events, God has engineered this eerie about-face. Just as Adam and Eve were faced with the promise of death while yet in the midst of a world filled with life eternal, we exist in a mirror existence, in which we're confronted with the promise of life eternal while yet in the midst of a world filled with death.

So, in response, you might say, "How interesting that you put it that way. Yes, I see that now. Just as we find it so difficult, living in today's world, to lay hold of God's promise of life when we've never known anything but death, it'd be just as difficult to grasp the idea of God's promise of death when Adam and Eve never knew anything but life. So, yes, if I were given the chance to act differently, I can see now, in a way I've never considered before: I'd do exactly what they did. I'm clear on that point. But what I'm not so clear on is: What's this got to do with our present investigation?"

"I'm so glad you asked," I'd reply. "Let me tell you, then."

The reason I've done all this is because, as I've previously stated, I'm hoping to provide an answer to the question of God's aloofness so as to accomplish two things and not just one. I hope to refute the argument of unbelievers who insist that suffering, disease, and death are irrefutable evidence of God's non-existence. And I hope to refute the argument of believers who doubt God's faithfulness when confronted by said evidence. And my answer, in light of this scene of Adam and Eve in the Garden of Eden, is this.

When God expelled them for eating the Forbidden Fruit, it wasn't just a punishment in the strictest sense of that word, as we normally understand it. By renouncing Adam and Eve's eternal nature and thus allowing mortality to infect the human race, God was also demonstrating that, for good or for bad, He'd be faithful to His word of promise. So, actually, as hard as it is for us to bear, the separation between God and us, which began on the day Adam and Eve were exiled, didn't occur because God is unfaithful but because He's absolutely faithful.

As a result of such an understanding, which turns the table on our typical view of the situation, suddenly suffering, disease, and death can no longer be seen as the result of God's disregard for humanity but, rather, they're the result of His abiding presence in His creation.

Now, just because mortality has entered the human experience, it doesn't mean that God is sitting back forever after and saying, "See, I told you so." It just means that when it comes to demonstrating His control over history to a skeptical world, He's faithful to His word, regardless of the consequences—both good and bad. And again, as harsh as this may seem on the surface, there's still the flipside to this reality.

As it turns out, suffering, disease, and death actually provide humanity with proof of God's faithfulness, although it's proof that's as painful and distressing as it is obvious and evident. Consequently, this realization should make it just as obvious and evident that God's promise of peace, health, and life will take place when acted upon, just as certainly as those that pertain to suffering, disease, and death.

In the end, such evidence flies in the face of both unbelievers, who seek to use their presence to dismiss God's existence, and believers, who question God's faithfulness because of them. Or, as *The Bible* portrays it, the same words bring life to some but death to others. The Apostle Paul put it this way:

> To God, we're a sweet fragrance of Christ. Not only to God and to those who are saved but also to those who are lost. To some, we bring the stench of death to death, whereas to others, we spread the scent of life to life…
>
> For godly sorrow produces repentance, leading to salvation, for which there's no need of repentance; but the world's grief leads only to death.
>
> *The Second Book of Corinthians*

What remains, then, when both sides have ceased their fruitless arguing and the dust has settled? What remains is an entirely new way to perceive suffering, disease, and death. Instead of seeing them as evidence of God's disregard for humanity, these terrors actually become shattering proofs that God is ever faithful to His word of promise, for good and for bad—to the chagrin of unbelievers everywhere and to the joy of believers for all time.

CHAPTER FIVE
A Tale of Two Worlds
(Because Only Through the Fall Could We Know What It Means to Be Truly Human)

> **MIND**, *a noun*
> **A mysterious form of matter secreted by the brain. Its chief activity consists in the endeavor to ascertain its own nature, the futility of the attempt being due to the fact that it has nothing but itself to know itself with.**
>
> *The Cynic's Word Book,* Ambrose Bierce

NOW THAT we've addressed how *The Bible* doesn't depict a perfect world inhabited by perfect people, let's see how Scripture reveals that this central fact of human existence doesn't diminish the perfection of God as Creator of the Universe. That's because without understanding why God was willing to unleash the more undesirable aspects of free will into the Universe, we can never appreciate why God continues to preserve and maintain free will despite the apparent liabilities that come with it, such as human suffering that inevitably leads to widespread cynicism.

So the question remains: Just because *The Bible* demonstrates that God is faithful and that our Universe speaks of His control, how does this explain why evil was allowed to enter our world in the first place? In short: Just because God is in control and is faithful, it still doesn't make up for the fact that He personally unleashed the ultimate monster—evil—upon an unsuspecting humanity. Whether that monster is seen in terms of death, Hell, and the grave, or darkness, sadness, and pain, the fact that God is to blame for the dire predicament we're in—quite apart from Adam's guilt in the whole debacle—undermines any of our bold pronouncements of "God is in control" and "God is faithful." Such is the power of that dreaded archenemy of humanity, such is its power that no vision of divine beauty and grace can withstand its corrosive sting, such is the power of cynicism.

Therefore, it's with the utmost urgency that I attempt to deliver a deathblow to such a one as cynicism, an enemy of such magnitude that it alone can single-handedly undermine every valiant effort offered by way of the promises of God. How, then, do we answer the ultimate question on the lips of anyone who has ever asked such an obvious question? Why, in fact, would a loving and compassionate God allow evil to enter a world with such potential for hope, truth, and beauty? Quite simply, God did it because He knew that in creating divinely-constituted beings like ourselves, the one thing He couldn't create—as a function of the God-like spark of free will—was both innocence *and* maturity at the same time in those beings *from the start*.

The only way to know what it means to be truly human—to be our "selves" in every sense of that word as opposed to the Great Other Who created us—we must experience firsthand the duality of God's Universe. But in order to do that—and herein lies the rub—one can't remain blissfully innocent forever. In other words, without being "cast out" of the womb of Eden, we'd never have known darkness, sadness, or pain, but ironically, without knowing any of these things, we'd never be able to realize our full potential as individuals made in God's image. Because without knowing darkness, we could never appreciate light; without knowing sadness, we could never experience happiness; without knowing pain, we could never embrace pleasure. Simply put, to go through life without experiencing such dualities would be like never living at all.

Fortunately, while God may have allowed suffering, disease, and death to enter the world, it hasn't prevented Him from also entering our world in a remarkable and mysterious way, to work out an end which could never have occurred had we remained ensconced in a permanent state of innocence. Even a confirmed cynic like Bierce saw something of this paradoxical truth, when he drew up the following scene:

> The Virtues chose Modesty to be their queen.
> "I didn't know that I was a virtue," she said. "Why didn't you choose Innocence?"
> "Because of her ignorance," they replied. "She knows nothing but that she is a virtue."
>
> *A Cynic Looks at Life*

Bottom line: A world filled with dualities—regardless of the pain they may bring—is still preferable to a world without them. Without the potential for disappointment or shame, there'd be no potential for hope or modesty. What's more, without disappointment, there'd be no need to become cynical about God's motives. And without cynicism, there wouldn't be so many people who question the motives of others, and, by extension, the ethical norms and values of society at large.

All things considered, then, it seems self-evident that instead of blaming God for all that we typically blame Him for, we should reconcile all such incongruities into a cohesive worldview. Rather than bemoan how difficult it is to accomplish such a task, let's assume that the foregoing facts of our existence aren't as irreconcilable as they appear at first glance. What have we got so far?

First, we saw how trying to explain the more inexplicable things in our world, like suffering, disease, and death, comes down to one's ability or inability to put in the hard work it takes to reconcile such conundrums. That's because doubt comes so much easier to humans than does certainty, which is why the happiest people in the world lean toward agnosticism rather than theism, and toward cynicism rather than hopefulness.

Second, we confronted the paradoxical quality of cynicism, which, even from a biblical point of view, is said to comprise a healthy form on one end of the spectrum and a malignant form at the other end. As such, we learned that any legitimate example of suspicion can be modified by introducing new facts, while cynicism is resistant to anything that contradicts its original position, leaving it impervious to rising above the merely suspicious.

Third, we recognized we're all in a similar situation where we're caught between two worlds as a result of God's gift of free will. What's more, this gift of freedom affords humanity a rare, double-edged opportunity: Depending on whether we act based on our certainty or our doubt, we uniquely manifest either the beauty and grandeur of God's original creation or the degradation and ugliness that tarnished it with the Fall of Man.

And finally, we came to grips with the question of why God allowed evil to enter the world, with His unleashing of free will into the Universe, and in answering that question based on the scriptural record, we came face to face with the fact that only through the tragedy of the Fall could we ever know fully what it means to be truly human.

That said, what remains is: How do we as a species determine the true nature of humanity's greatest enemy? Because as it turns out, the enemy isn't suffering, disease, or death; it's not God, or the devil, or our free will; it's not ourselves, or our families, or other human beings; it's not our institutions, or our government. The greatest enemy of humanity isn't even sin—if, that is, you believe in the efficacy of the sacrifice of Christ on Calvary. That's because the Scriptures are clear: "Without faith, it's impossible to please God," and, "Wherever sin abounds, grace abounds much more." Based on these assurances, then, we understand what really alienates us from God's grace, peace, and truth: The real enemy is cynicism.

That's because cynicism eats at the root of the only thing that can overcome any obstacle that stands between us and God's love and power. Therefore, it behooves us to further analyze how cynicism alienates us from all that God has provided us. After all, the life of faith isn't just about trying to be a good person, then dying and going to Heaven; it's about fulfilling the prayer of Jesus Who taught us to pray that God's will be done on Earth as it is on Heaven.

What does that mean? It means that as Christians we're to be meaningful members of a family, of a church, of a society, and thus through these earthly vehicles, the heavenly realm of God's Kingdom is made manifest through our very lives. As such, we have to be on guard and understand just how cynicism is the greatest impediment to connecting with God and thus our ultimate purpose in life.

TO BEGIN WITH, cynicism's most obvious effect on humanity is how it colors the way we relate to a world that for all intents and purposes seems devoid of God's presence. Yet even in the midst of this perceived absence of the Divine, the God of *The Bible* challenges us to see beyond this condition, to see the real truth of the matter. As it is written:

> The Heavens declare the glory of God; the skies proclaim the work of His hands. Day after day, they pour forth speech; night after night, they reveal knowledge.
>
> Without speech or language, without a sound to be heard, their voice has gone out into all the Earth, their words to the ends of the world.
>
> *The Book of Psalms*

As such, God may not seem to be in our midst due to the fallout of Adam's forfeiture of that first contract, but that has never stopped the reality of God from manifesting in the Universe. From time immemorial, one of the primary messages of Scripture is that, in addition to the written word given to humanity, there is the grandeur and beauty of the natural world to demonstrate—even articulate, if you will—God's existence.

> For God shows His anger from Heaven against evil people who suppress the truth in wickedness. They know the truth about God, as He's made it evident to them, because ever since the world was created, people have seen the Earth and sky. By way of everything that God has made, they can clearly see His invisible qualities, His eternal power, and divine nature, so they have no excuse for not knowing Him.
>
> Yes, they knew God, but they wouldn't worship Him as God or even give Him thanks, so they began to think up foolish ideas of what God was like. As a result, their minds became dark and confused. Claiming to be wise, they instead became fools. Instead of worshiping the Living God, they worshiped idols made to look like mere people and birds and animals and reptiles.

So God abandoned them to do whatever shameful things their hearts desired. As a result, they did vile and degrading things with each other's bodies. They traded the truth about God for a lie.

So they worshiped and served the things that God created instead of the Creator Himself, Who alone is worthy of eternal praise! Amen.

The Book of Romans

In this passage, we see how, since the beginning of creation, there has been something within nature itself that can impart a knowledge of God but that has, for the most part, been actively suppressed. Here we see one of the most succinct expressions of what happens when the cynical mind reinterprets what it sees and hears. Like the Pharisees who could see nothing marvelous or awe-inspiring in the raising of Lazarus, there will always be those who look upon the world around them who likewise can't see beyond it to the One Who created it. Instead of being in awe of the Creator, they're fooled into thinking the creatures are worthy of the adoration that is due only to Him.

This, then, sets off a chain reaction of tragic proportions that can't help but end in disaster, because an awareness that the natural world imparts a knowledge of God is, in turn, critical to one's acceptance or rejection of God's written word itself. What do I mean by that?

Well, consider the extent to which you either accept or reject the idea that the natural world around you reveals God's reality. Then ask yourself: To what extent does that acceptance or rejection translate into your view concerning God's ability or inability to communicate via the written word? I know in my own experience the two ideas go hand in hand. First, I consider the intricacy and immensity of the natural world, and as a result, I can only conclude it's impossible that it all came into being spontaneously and independent of a Divine Designer. Then, I consider that if a God can orchestrate all this, then He certainly has the power to communicate with His own creatures, quite apart from the implications of the Fall of Man.

I mean, seriously, who but the most cynical among us can't deduce that the One Who created our mouths, our eyes, and our ears can't communicate what He wants us to know. But once we firmly settle this idea in our thinking, that God's revelation in nature undergirds His written revelation, we can overcome any number of objections that challenge a belief in *The Bible*.

Consider just some of the objections of those who insist the Scriptures aren't the product of divine inspiration: *The Bible* is full of contradictions, say critics, and is therefore unreliable. These contradictions—contained in both Testaments, Old and New—range from the discrepancies in the various historical accounts that seem to be described in such a haphazard manner, to the incongruities in God's judgments that seem so at odds with our own sense of justice. As for the discrepancies in historical events, critics cite the jumbled accounts describing the creation of the world, Noah's role in the Great Flood, and the life, death, and resurrection of Jesus. As for the incongruities in God's judgments, critics cite that God violated basic principles of justice in destroying the whole Earth's population in the Flood, in the extermination of seven nations in the Conquest of Canaan, and in the cataclysmic events described in *The Book of Revelation*.

Now admittedly, these discrepancies and incongruities do seem to represent plausible objections as to the status of *The Bible* as being the inspired word of God. No doubt, they do exist; and I'd certainly never suggest that they aren't there for all to see. No doubt it is just these discrepancies and incongruities that had Bierce describe history as "an account, mostly false, of events, mostly unimportant, which are brought about by rulers, mostly knaves, and soldiers, mostly fools." However, I would suggest there's another way to interpret said discrepancies and incongruities, because like so much in the way of properly understanding truth, the most important thing to remember is: To what extent are we examining these accounts in their proper context?

A well-known axiom states: "Text without context is error." And so, a parallel to such thinking could read: "Evidence apart from its proper context is erroneous." Certainly, anyone who has had the awesome responsibility of sitting on a jury in a murder trial would agree that no verdict is a just verdict unless all the evidence is considered and not simply that which is circumstantial in nature. This is never more true than when considering the judgments that are leveled at *The Bible*. Yet in nearly every case, when evidence disputing the veracity of Scripture is offered, it is always circumstantial in nature and never offered in the full context in which it actually exists.

What's more, in determining the context of a given matter, it's critically important to remember how the attitude of the observer has the ultimate power to determine the outcome of one's investigation upon being exposed to said context.

That said, let's see how all of the preceding ideas come into play in trying to determine if the Scriptures are reliable or not. First, to what extent are we looking at these biblical contradictions in the proper context, historically and ethically speaking? Second, to what extent does our own tendency toward cynicism shape our understanding of these discrepancies and incongruities? And third, how likely is it that a Being capable of creating our Universe can also provide a reliable written record of His will for humanity?

AS FOR THE so-called "discrepancies" in historical events in *The Bible*, let me point out the most important factor in judging the reliability of history: Historical accounts are never comprised of a single, monolithic narrative that is either true or false. Our knowledge of history—even biblical history—is, by its very nature, always a confluence of eyewitness accounts gathered from a multitude of sources. From this variety of perspectives, we derive a particular sense of that history, in which a core narrative emerges that contains some elements that are more consistent with actual events, while other elements of that narrative provide peripheral accounts that are less consistent. However, just because history is shown to be a confluence of subplots within the matrix of a larger plotline, that doesn't mean that the reporting of given events are unreliable simply because they were described in ways that were more or less accurate.

Imagine if we were expected to believe that certain historical events, such as the Pilgrims' landing at Plymouth Rock or Washington's crossing of the Delaware, were untrue just because some aspects of their recounting were exaggerated or embellished. So when critics seek to undermine our confidence in *The Bible*, they seem to be coming at it with a disjointed logic. In my view, it seems to be yet another symptom of cynicism at work. It seems to me that it's not so much that the particular events didn't happen the way they're described in Scripture. Their real agenda is to undermine the theological position that *The Bible* is the inspired word of God. What really bothers them is the self-proclaimed contention that:

> All Scripture is God-breathed and is useful for instruction, for conviction, for correction, and for training in righteousness, so that the people of God may be complete, fully equipped for every good work.
>
> *The Second Book of Timothy*

Accordingly, if critics can point out what they view as contradictions, then they feel justified in ridiculing anyone who believes in a book that contains errors. But the truth is, they should think twice before throwing stones at others, because if they ever applied the same standard to their history books, they'd be shocked to find that they were riddled with just as many discrepancies and incongruities.

The issue with attacking *The Bible*, then, rests not so much on the fact that its historical narratives incorporate a variety of eyewitness accounts, which by their very nature introduce discrepancies into those accounts. The real issue is whether the Scriptures can be relied on even though they contain accounts that are just as susceptible to the inherent limitations of human perception.

After all, even most believers understand that *The Bible* wasn't handed down from On-High in its present form as if written by a single hand. Even they understand that anyone who tries to destroy their confidence in it can only do so by way of a Straw Man argument. First, critics insist that the biblical writers themselves declared the Scriptures to be infallible in every way and with every translation—as opposed to later generations of theologians who have. Then, having created an impossible position to maintain, the critics declare victory over the Straw Man—who never existed in the first place—when they find the inevitable contradictions in Scripture. Unfortunately, just as many believers aggravate the situation because they feel they'd be betraying God if they acknowledged even the slightest possibility of errors because *The Bible* is a compendium of books written, edited, translated, and reproduced by so many hands down through the corridors of time.

In this, the biblical writers are just like those proverbial Blind Men who, in the famous parable, sought to understand the nature of the Elephant with which they were interacting, each from their own point of view. To the extent that one of them was touching but a single aspect of the Elephant, for them, that was the reality of the whole. To the one who was touching the trunk, it *was* a snake; to the one who was holding the leg, it *was* a tree; and to the one who was holding the tail, it *was* a rope. By virtue of the form of reality that that man was interacting with, that became the sum of his experience and so it was the "truth" for him.

Never mind that the remarkable thing about *The Bible* is that despite it being the product of a multiplicity of perspectives it still bears the obvious stamp of a singular mind, a singular theme, a singular plan. Never mind that God's other purpose for His written record is to demonstrate that in Him and through Him He could protect and perpetuate a knowledge of His will for all generations.

But thank God, not everyone goes through life imprisoned by a cynical mind, because those who have thrown off those shackles clearly see the Straw Man for who he is: God's message isn't diminished just because it's been mediated through the eyes and ears and mouths of mere humans—humans which, by the way, just happen to have been created in God's image. No, that criticism will only work on those who can't think for themselves and who are themselves captured by the voice of the Straw Man who claims what the Scriptures have never tried to claim, although the devil and his minions have rejoiced in it being proclaimed. While the enemies of truth would have us believe that every historical account in *The Bible* must be perfect in every way—or else it's invalid—the writers themselves were quite content to admit to the veiled nature of the truth they were grappling with. As it is written:

> For now we see through a glass, darkly; but someday face to face. Now I know only in part; but one day I will fully know even as I also am known.
>
> *The First Book of Corinthians*

So, as well-meaning as believers are in saying there's no possibility of biblical errors creeping in, it only sets the stage for the very thing that I'm suggesting undoes God's efforts in providing us with a written record: False expectations inevitably lead to disappointment, which in turn leads to disillusionment, which in turn leads to widespread loss of faith. In short: It's the perfect recipe for cynicism. Far better to embrace the truth of what it means to be fallen creatures in a fallen world—not without hope, though not fully capable of being perfect in an imperfect world. Far better to face the truth and resist being intimidated by a world that insists that, to be deemed "God-breathed, useful for instruction, conviction, correction, and training in righteousness," Scripture has to be perfect in every way.

Trust me when I say, God won't fall off His throne if you put away the childish notion that *The Bible* is perfect in every way, any more than He'd fall off if you were heard to say that the present creation isn't perfect in every way. Put simply, *The Bible* is magnificent, to be sure, but not flawless; majestic, without a doubt, but not infallible; sublime in all its depths, yes, but not without its blemishes. Yet together, hand in hand, God's word in nature and God's word in written form still reveal exactly what God intended them to reveal, even in their marred state that leaves them both yearning for the day when the children of God finally witness the consummation of the ages.

But until then, they do speak—just as loudly and as clearly as is needed until that future day.

CHAPTER SIX

A Lack of Perspective
(Because Every Story in The Bible Needs to Be Told in Its Proper Context)

> **EFFECT,** *a noun*
> "The second of two phenomena which always occur together in the same order. The first, called a Cause, is said to generate the other—which is no more sensible than it would be for one who has never seen a dog except in pursuit of a rabbit to declare the rabbit the cause of the dog."
>
> *The Cynic's Word Book,* Ambrose Bierce

AS FOR THE so-called "incongruities" in God's judgments in *The Bible,* let me point out the most important factor in judging the quality of justice: We're never on shakier ground, morally speaking, than when we, as a modern audience, presume to examine the past through the lens of our own perspective. When this happens, it becomes almost impossible to arrive at any accurate conclusions about the past, as is the case when we make moral judgments of people who lived in a time when such practices as polygamy, incest, and slavery were considered normal. One may accuse me of being inhuman or uneducated but in the context of moral judgment, such accusations exist more in the realm of feeling than of fact.

As for the facts concerning God's judgments of Adam and Eve's descendants, we must first ask the question: What is the actual context of humanity's predicament as members of a race of outcasts of Eden? Remember how we learned that, based on a biblical view of such matters and not merely a humanistic view, the presence of suffering, disease, and death didn't occur simply as a punishment. It was also a form of God being faithful to His promise that Adam and Eve would die if they partook of the Forbidden Fruit, which in turn laid the foundation for our hope in God's promise of eternal life to those who trust Him. But to the cynical mind, such things are sheer nonsense and thus the furthest thing from their minds; and so they'd be the first to conclude that all suffering, disease, and death for any reason is unjust according to their so-called "human standards of morality."

Seen in the context of the biblical record, though, we might finally face two inescapable conclusions: First, God can never be found guilty in any court of law—human or cosmic—of any human death, any more than you or I could be found guilty of a crime that we never committed. And second, since so much of human suffering is the result of our own actions, we must now acknowledge the absurdity of applying our standard of morality to indict God for such results.

Next, we need to analyze the context of those other events in which critics of *The Bible* insist that God acted in a savage and criminal manner. First, we're told God acted barbarically when he destroyed an entire world in the Great Flood. Just think of it, they exclaim: Every man, woman, and child on the planet, killed! Every animal, every living creature on the planet, killed! Did they all really deserve to die so horribly?

Admittedly, on the surface, asking such a question does

seem warranted. On the surface, that is. Unfortunately, biblical stories like these have always been the greatest source of cynicism when we consider just how much they contradict the idea of a loving and merciful God. But just as unfortunate is the fact that when it comes to condemning God for such apparently monstrous actions, upon further review the real monster turns out to be of a completely different species. That's because if we read the Scriptures for ourselves and actually take the time to put the story of Noah's Flood in its proper context, we can't help but see it an entirely different way. Let's see what I mean by that.

According to tradition, we're told that God's judgment was the result of humanity becoming so debased and evil that the Lord finally got fed up and pronounced worldwide doom by deluge. As it is written:

> Then the Lord saw that the wickedness of man was great in the Earth, and that every intent of the thoughts of his heart was continually evil. And the Lord was sorry that He'd made man on the Earth, and He was grieved in His heart. So the Lord said, "I will destroy man whom I've created from the face of the Earth, both man and beast, creeping thing and birds of the air, for I'm sorry that I've made them."
>
> *The Book of Genesis*

Pretty harsh stuff, if you ask me. And remember: I'm a believer; I'm no cynic. I figure God must have had a pretty good reason for doing what He did. But one thing I can tell you: I've always been suspicious that there's something missing in this account that we're not being told about. I mean, really, it's not like God is that shocked at the sight of human sin. This is something we've already discussed in an earlier chapter. If human sin was so abhorrent and despicable to God, and so deserving of such cataclysmic judgment, then why didn't Jesus respond in a similar manner in the presence of prostitutes and tax collectors? So we know there must be another component to this story that could fill in the missing piece of this puzzle. If only we knew where to find it, then maybe the cynical mind would feel less justified in disparaging God for sending the Flood. But what could it be?

Well, as it turns out, the component we're looking for can be found in some biblical clues that have been staring us in the face all along. Too bad, though, that our old nemesis cynicism has had its way in obscuring a view of those clues so that traditional biblical history no longer makes clear what that component is. To see what I mean by that just look at the verses that lead up to those we're most familiar with—believers and unbelievers alike.

> Now it came to pass, when men began to multiply on the face of the Earth, and daughters were born to them, that the sons of God saw the daughters of men, that they were beautiful; and they took wives for themselves of all whom they chose.
>
> And the Lord said, "My Spirit won't strive with humans forever, because they're only flesh; yet their days shall be one hundred and twenty years." There were giants on the Earth in those days, and afterward, when the sons of God came in to the daughters of men, they bore children to them. Those were the mighty men who were of old, men of renown.
>
> *The Book of Genesis*

So there we have it, the hidden clue we need to put this story into its proper context, one which is typically glossed over due to the subtlety of the *Genesis* account.

"But wait," you might interject, "didn't you say that the real culprit, as usual, was cynicism? How does that come into play with the traditional reading of these verses?"

To which I'd reply: "It does so by way of Moses deciding to leave something out in his rendition of Noah's Flood."

"Moses' rendition? What's that supposed to mean? Is there another rendition of this story that we don't know about?"

As a matter of fact, yes, there is. And it just so happens that the reason most believers in *The Bible* are unaware of this rendition is due to the cynicism of several Church Fathers who banned it because they disapproved of its telling of the Flood, which just happened to provide the real reason why God destroyed the world's population the way He did.

First, let's highlight the hidden clue I alluded to earlier, then we'll examine that clue in light of this other rendition of which I spoke, and hopefully in doing so, we'll arrive at a brand-new view of why God did what He did. In doing so, we might also debunk the debunkers of *The Bible* who think they're justified in claiming that God's actions are inconsistent with the most basic human values that anyone can see should be upheld, even by God.

> There were giants on the Earth in those days, and afterward, when the sons of God came in to the daughters of men, they bore children to them. Those were the mighty men who were of old, men of renown.
>
> *The Book of Genesis*

There's our clue, then: "When the sons of God came in to the daughters of men, children were born to them." But not just any children; these children—as attested to in both renditions we'll examine—became giants, or, as in many of our translations of Scripture tell it: *Nephilim*. It was these *Nephilim*, in fact, these mighty men of old, of renown, that were the real reason why God unleashed the Flood. And we know this because of that other rendition I described, which is found in an ancient text long said to have been written by none other than the seventh son of Adam—Enoch—the man who walked and talked with God and whom God eventually "took," says *The Book of Hebrews*, "because he pleased the Lord." That text is known as *The Book of Enoch*, or *First Enoch*, and its author described in full detail what Moses only alluded to in his rendition in *Genesis*.

> And it came to pass when the children of men had multiplied in those days that beautiful daughters were born to them. And the angels, the sons of Heaven, saw and lusted after them, and said to one another: "Come, let us choose wives from among the children of men and beget us children."
>
> And the women became pregnant, and they bare great giants, whose height was three thousand ells and who consumed all the acquisitions of men. And when men could no longer sustain them, the giants turned against them and devoured mankind.
>
> And they began to sin against birds, and beasts, and reptiles, and fish, and to devour one another's flesh, and drink their blood. Then the Earth laid accusation against the lawless ones.
>
> *The First Book of Enoch*

Far from blaming mere human sin for the Great Flood—without diminishing the tragic stain of sin in any way—we see from this: The real reason for sending the Flood was to remove the *Nephilim* from the Earth and not simply as a punishment for human sin. And while one may question the validity of such a claim, depending on one's tendency toward cynicism, it certainly demonstrates the importance of telling every story in *The Bible* in its proper context, without which we're driven to a far different view of God's motives for doing what He's done throughout history.

Another example of this confusion as to the right or wrong of God's actions in relation to our human understanding of morality and justice is seen in God's ordering the Israelites to conquer the seven nations of Canaan. In the case of the Conquest of Canaan, however, we don't need to look any further than the canonical version of *The Bible* to put this story in its proper context. Unbeknownst to critics of Scripture who ridicule God as being malicious, callous, monstrous—you name it—in His brutal act of ordering the genocide of seven nations, you must first understand that their extermination was actually the result of a long-delayed judgment first alluded to in *Genesis*.

At the time, Abraham was still wandering through the land of Canaan as a stranger many years before he and Sarah ever had the promised son that God spoke of. Upon making a burnt offering to God, a deep sleep fell upon Abraham, and suddenly terror and darkness overwhelmed him. It was then that God promised Abraham that someday his descendants would possess the very land in which he now wandered as a mere outsider. But that someday, said God, would occur only after "the iniquity of the Amorites was complete."

This idea was further illustrated many years later when the Israelites were on the verge of entering the Promised Land, and Moses told the people:

> When the Lord your God has driven them out before you, don't say to yourselves, "Because of our righteousness the Lord has brought us in to possess this land." Rather, the Lord is driving out these nations before you because of their wickedness.
>
> It's not because of your righteousness or uprightness of heart that you're going in to possess their land, but it's because of their wickedness that

the Lord your God is driving out these nations before you, to keep the promise He swore to your fathers—to Abraham, Isaac, and Jacob. Understand, then, that it isn't because of your righteousness that the Lord your God is giving you this good land to possess, because you're a stubborn people.

The Book of Deuteronomy

So you see when critics of *The Bible* try to shame anyone into thinking God's actions are inconsistent with human standards of morality or justice, they can only maintain their moral high ground by isolating events in Scripture to make others think God is acting arbitrarily, when in fact He's acting quite consistently. In this case, God, just as He had done with Sodom and Gomorrah, gave the inhabitants of Canaan four full generations to reform their evil ways, at which time God executed judgment upon them, just as Israel and Judah would one day be punished by the Assyrians and Babylonians, each in their own time and according to their set time of judgment and punishment.

Of course, the real irony in critics insisting that *The Bible* depicts God acting in opposition to civilized standards of morality is: If there is a Supreme Being, then who is to say which standard is the correct standard by which to judge His actions? This was, after all, the dilemma that Job's friends faced when they rebuked him for what they saw as just punishment according to their view of divine justice. In their eyes, although Job had always seemed to be a God-fearing man and above reproach, his suffering must have been the result of some secret sin in his life.

The only problem was, while Job's friends seemed justified in their opinion that Job was personally responsible for his suffering, their pat judgment turned out to be completely unfounded. Not because Job's friends lacked an adequate knowledge of morality in their day. If anything, they were overly sensitized to its demands, albeit in an overly simplistic way. In their view, justice came in only two colors, black and white. The way they saw it: Good things happen to people who do good, and bad things happen to those who do bad. What could be more basic than that?

The error in their judgment, then, regarding the cause of Job's suffering, stemmed from their lack of perspective in the matter. As such, they failed to see the "big picture," which is just another way of saying that in Job's case: "Evidence apart from its proper context is erroneous."

To understand the proper context, by which to correctly judge the players in this scenario, we need to look at what Job or his friends could never have known at the time, and what we only know because the writer of this story made it known to us. As it is written:

> One day, when the sons of God came to present themselves before the Lord, Satan also came among them.
>
> Then the Lord asked Satan, "Where have you been lately?"
>
> And Satan said to the Lord, "I've been traveling back and forth about the Earth, and walking every which way."
>
> And the Lord asked Satan, "Have you considered my servant Job? There's no one quite like him on Earth—a blameless and upright man, who fears God and turns away from evil."
>
> Then Satan replied, "Of course Job reveres you, and for good reason. You've placed a hedge around him, his house, and everything he has! You've blessed the work of his hands, and all his possessions have increased in the land. But just watch: Stretch out your hand and touch all that he has, and he'll curse you to your face."

> And the Lord said, "Very well, then. Everything he has is yours now. But see to it that you do no harm to him."
>
> *The Book of Job*

From that point on, Job was struck by one disaster after another. First, raiding marauders stole his oxen and donkeys, and killed many of his servants. Then fire fell from the sky and burned up his sheep and many more of his servants. Next, a devastating wind blew down the house where his children were dining, killing everyone inside except for the servant who alone survived to report the bad news to Job. Despite all those tragedies, Job never blamed God for his predicament.

After that, God then allowed Satan to up the ante, so to speak, and Job's suffering intensified, thanks to Satan's attack on him personally. Job's body was smitten with painful boils; then along came his friends to add insult to injury. They did their best not to vex him with their prejudices and assumptions as to why he was enduring such misery and pain, but add to it they did. They tried to withhold their judgment, but the temptation to criticize him was just too great. Then Eliphaz, the Temanite, said to Job:

> Stop and think! Do the innocent die? When have the upright been destroyed? My experience shows that those who plant trouble and cultivate evil will harvest the same.
>
> A breath from God destroys them. They vanish in a blast of His anger...
>
> But consider the joy of those who are corrected by God! Don't despise the Almighty's discipline when you sin. Although He wounds, He also bandages. He strikes, but His hands also heal.
>
> *The Book of Job*

Like his misery and pain, Job took his friend's remarks in stride as long as he could, before finally replying:

> Honest words can be painful, but what do your criticisms amount to? Do you think your words are convincing when you disregard my cry of desperation?
>
> You'd even send an orphan into slavery or sell a friend. Look at me! Would I lie to your face? Stop assuming my guilt, because I haven't done anything wrong. You think I'm lying? Don't I know the difference between right and wrong?
>
> *The Book of Job*

Imagine a world—then and now—where what you think about right and wrong no longer matters, when everything you think you know about divine justice and divine punishment is turned upside down. That indeed was Job's world in that moment, as well as countless others ever since Job's day, which is why Job's dilemma still speaks to us who are likewise familiar with that upside-down world.

And just when you thought people like Job's friends were relics of the past, today's cynics step right up to echo their prejudices and assumptions—some of which are similarly aimed at our perceived shortcomings and failures, and some at God's perceived apathy and callousness.

But as for Job, although he had no idea why he was suffering, he still knew God well enough to not abandon his trust in the divine will. In short, while Job could have viewed the world through the lens of his friends' cynicism, he chose to view it through the lens of his own hope. Still struggling in his anguish, Job however began to describe the real crux of the matter, in answer to both the cynics in his day and ours, concerning any human judgment that would criticize God in what He does in relation to His own creation. Said Job:

> If someone wanted to take God to court, would it be possible to answer Him even once in a thousand times?
>
> For God is so wise and so mighty. Who's ever challenged Him successfully? Without warning, He moves the mountains, overturning them in His anger. He shakes the Earth from its place, and its foundations tremble...
>
> If He snatches someone in death, who can stop Him?
>
> Who dares to ask, "What are You doing?" If it's a question of strength, He's the strong one. If it's a matter of justice, who dares summon Him to court?
>
> *The Book of Job*

In many ways, this exchange between Job and his friends—as to who's guilty, or who's innocent, and why—provides a paradigm for anyone who thinks they're an expert on the moral foundations by which to judge God. And when I say anyone, I do mean anyone—the hardcore cynic and the merely suspicious alike. Think you've figured out the true meaning of justice? Think you're qualified to pass judgment on God, and how He treats the human race? Think again.

From out of the whirlwind, the Lord answered Job and Job's friends; and He answered the hardcore cynic and the merely suspicious, too:

> Who is questioning My wisdom with such ignorant words? Brace yourself like a man, because I have some questions for you, and you must answer them.
> Where were you when I laid the foundations

of the Earth? Tell me, if you know so much. Who determined its dimensions and stretched out the surveying line? What supports its foundations, and who laid its cornerstone as the morning stars sang together and all the sons of God shouted for joy?

Who kept the sea inside its boundaries as it burst from the womb, and as I clothed it with clouds and wrapped it in thick darkness? For I locked it behind barred gates, limiting its shores. I said, "This far and no farther will you come. Here your proud waves must stop!"

Have you ever commanded the morning to appear and caused the dawn to rise in the east? Have you made daylight spread to the far reaches of the Earth, to bring an end to the night's wickedness? As the light approaches, the Earth takes shape like clay pressed beneath a seal; it's robed in brilliant colors. The light disturbs the wicked, and stops the arm that is raised in violence.

The Book of Job

Notice how God doesn't reply here to His creatures in purely moralistic terms as we might expect. He doesn't go into a convoluted discussion about right and wrong, justice and injustice, as, say, a judge who is trying to convince a jury of his or her moral authority. No, God completely bypassed any such line of reasoning and instantly cut the legs out from underneath anyone trying to intimidate Him for what He does. "You presume to question what I do in regard to My creatures? Really. So tell Me: Where were you when I laid the foundations of the Earth?" In essence, God says, "While you may think your arguments about right and wrong, about justice and injustice, are correct, you're ignoring several other key points to those arguments: When was the last time you commanded the morning to appear? When have you ever made the daylight to end the night's wickedness?"

In framing His rebuttal this way, God is saying to the cynical mind the same thing that Job said to his presumptuous friends: "You offer your honest words of criticism, but what do they amount to when, in offering them, you ignore someone's desperate cries? At least when I pass judgment, I don't just talk about mercy while withholding it, as you do. When the night's wickedness prevails because of Satan's reign of terror upon Adam's children, I alone cause the dawn to rise in the east. Look how the light approaches, and in doing so, I alone disturb the wicked and stop the arm of violence."

So, whether in the case of Job's friends in their day or critics of *The Bible* in ours, the cynical mind always criticizes what it doesn't really understand, in terms of what it thinks it knows. In disregarding the genuine context of a given matter, they are thus arguing from a position of willing ignorance. And in every case—past, present, and future—when considering God's actions regarding His creatures, we must always remember the preceding facts when judging those actions, even when it tweaks the nose of anyone who claims to be morally superior to God Who alone sets the standard for right and wrong, justice and injustice.

Finally, when we do abandon our human prejudices in presuming to judge God, we're able then to throw off the shackles of this dying world that only appears to be devoid of the divine presence but which merely waits for us to look in hope beyond the veil of tears. And in that simple act of surrender, we lay hold of a new view of the world that ultimately sees the wickedness of night give way to the light of a new dawn.

CHAPTER SEVEN

A Recipe for Cynicism
(Because Dreams and Reality Rarely Coincide in the Way We Expect Them To)

> **PRESENT,** *a noun*
> "That part of eternity dividing the domain of disappointment from the realm of hope."
>
> *The Cynic's Word Book,* Ambrose Bierce

THERE'S AN old adage that says, "Some people will cut their nose off just to spite their face." Those are the same people who look upon the beauty and grandeur of the creation but don't see the presence of God. They only see His absence. They don't marvel at the mystery of life; they only groan at the stench of death. No doubt this is a residual effect of the Fall of Man, but as we've tried to demonstrate throughout this work, it's also a residual effect of embracing cynicism as a way of life. Because as tragic as the presence of death in this world is, when seen through the lens of hope, our eyes are opened to a brand-new way of viewing one of humanity's most dreaded enemies. That's because when we examine the present creation in its totality, we don't just see life that inevitably succumbs to death;

we also see abundant evidence for death that inevitably gives way to rebirth.

But before I dive into this much-overlooked aspect of the creation, I first need to highlight another way that cynicism colors our worldview, and more specifically, the way it colors our Western view of the world. That's because the important thing to remember about cynicism is that it always manifests as a result of hope disappointed. By that I mean, if you examine the worldview of various cultures throughout history, one can't help noticing that the more a particular culture seeks to manipulate the environment, the more pessimistic that culture becomes in regard to the results of that controlling effort.

As such, the Western approach to mastering the environment, with its emphasis on the scientific method, has both blessed and cursed humanity at large. In many ways, it opened the door to monumental leaps forward in food production, transportation, manufactured goods, health care, and the like. But because of the apparently limitless potential of scientific progress, in terms of economic and personal growth, the backlash of human failure inevitably led to widespread cynicism in the West. But rather than see the problem as a function of human frailty, critics insist the Industrial Revolution, as it came to be called, is the root cause of the disenfranchisement, disillusionment, and dehumanization of the individual. And while this failure may seem like it can rightly be blamed on so-called "Western progress," I'd suggest, in light of what we've examined so far, there's another culprit that's much more worthy of blame.

I'd suggest the presumed evils of scientific progress—that is to say, the disenfranchisement, disillusionment, and dehumanization of the individual—aren't by-products of the Industrial Revolution itself. I'd suggest they're by-products of hope disappointed, which, in the case of scientific progress, is a hope unlike any other in the history of human achievement. To demonstrate what I mean by this all one has to do is remember the old black-and-white movie reels we were shown in school about the wonderful world of the future, full of flying cars and automated supercities of tomorrow. According to those charming little science fantasies, our future was already supposed to be filled with boundless conveniences, prosperity, and happiness by now.

Never mind that our present world, of 2023 A.D., is actually overflowing with technological wizardry. Never mind that previous generations would think us mad if we told them of a world connected with jumbo jets, smartphones, and the Internet. Yet despite all this, and more, we can't help but be disillusioned by the huge gap between economic wealth and human happiness. That's because while the scientific method opened new doors to new possibilities for the future, and the Industrial Revolution provided new methods to make those new possibilities a reality, the fact remained that people were still required to work and sweat and perform the new tasks without which the new future would never become that reality.

But because dreams and reality rarely coincide in the way we expect them to, no one could have predicted the kind of division of labor that became the hallmark of the Industrial Age, where new technologies and methods forever changed the nature of work. Whereas in previous generations, craftspeople were responsible for producing an entire product, such as shoes or clothes or vehicles, the new methodology confined workers to performing narrowly specified and repetitive tasks that severely diminished one's satisfaction in a job well done.

As such, there was quite an unexpected reversal of fortunes: new technologies and methods did free innumerable individuals from generations of inescapable familial vocations and allowed for unprecedented levels of upward mobility. However, the price of this new potential for breaking the bonds of medieval guilds and generational immobility was simply a different kind of servitude "on the other side of the street," as it were, in service of the new factories and corporations. And if that's true, then critics of the Industrial Revolution don't have a leg to stand on when they attack our modern way of life as opposed to the old, because whether you preferred life before or after the new potential for upward mobility, everyone still lives, works, and dies within the same basic matrix of how people "make a living."

In changing how we look at this Western worldview, then, we see that traditional interpretations don't always hold up under scrutiny. As usual, it's so much easier to doubt the motives of those who are presumed to be nothing more than greedy capitalists. Instead of seeing the Fall of Man and the subsequent penchant for human sin as the real cause of disenfranchisement, disillusionment, and dehumanization, many people try to blame everything *but* the Fall and sin. And in doing so, I'd suggest that those who take this route are merely embracing what I'm calling the joy of cynicism, because in the end it's much easier to blame what you don't understand.

In this case, it's easier to blame factory owners and corporate leaders than all the other underlying factors that first contributed to the Industrial Revolution. If you want to find the truly guilty parties in the equation, then why not blame the consumers who relentlessly demand better and cheaper products faster and more efficiently? After all, without the demand, there'd be no one clamoring to provide the supply, right?

To the left, we have the typical citizen who's dazzled by the prospects of a future filled with science and progress; to the right, we have the typical worker who's captured by both the dream of a brighter personal tomorrow and a better job than his or her parents; and in the middle, we have the typical critic who's trying to make sense of forces beyond their capacity to grasp so they hurl their well-intentioned accusations in every direction.

Let's face it, then, all things considered: When it comes to creating a surefire recipe for cynicism, you can't find one better than in a world that can't possibly live up to the promises and expectations sold to us by pseudo-scientific salesmen. What's more, if we could devise a law to measure the impact of cynicism, you couldn't miss with the following formula:

> The more certain we are that something will happen, the more debilitating is our disappointment when that something fails to materialize in the way we expected it.

What do we have, then, in the final analysis? We have hope disappointed to the left, we have hope disappointed to the right, and we have hope disappointed in the middle. But what do you expect? We're all human, right? And if we're human, then our lives are inevitably full of disappointments. On the other hand, if we're human, then we also have that other side of our nature, a bright side, to counterbalance our dark side. Yes, as fallen beings living in a fallen world, we do tend toward cynicism by nature, but just as importantly, we still possess that other aspect of our being which remains in us as a function of our original creation in God's image.

That said, let's return to our present quest, that of determining the extent to which we so easily dismiss God's presence in His creation despite His reality being fully expressed through it. We'll also look at this dismissal in terms of the joy of cynicism, which describes how much easier it is to see the world in atheistic terms rather than theistically, as well as the formula, or recipe, for cynicism, which predicts the likelihood of seeing the world through cynical eyes whenever we exaggerate what life should be like if only our utopian dreams would come true.

LONG BEFORE Western progressivism took hold and long before westerners succumbed to modern cynicism, another form of presumption crept into the world. It was said that God gave Adam and his descendants dominion and authority over all creation, of those things on the Earth and above the Earth. Quite a lofty commission to live up to, to be sure, but commit to the task they did. The great irony in such a commission, though, was that Adam and his descendants conveniently neglected the fact that when God originally ordained them to be lords and masters of creation, Adam had yet to fall from grace and was still functioning under the lordship of the Master of creation.

Could this all-important fact of Adam's altered constitution be why our lofty potential for world domination has been repeatedly frustrated throughout the long ages of history? As usual, one needs to be careful to avoid setting goals too far above one's genuine capabilities. Expect too much, assume too much, and you inevitably find yourself a victim of your own expectations and assumptions. And that, as we're presently discovering, is the perfect recipe for cynicism.

Case in point: Let's revisit that classic scenario in which a mob of ambitious upstarts convinced themselves they could actually build a tower high enough to reach Heaven. No doubt, Noah and his family still remembered the bittersweet experience of being the only family in all the Earth to survive the Great Flood. No longer were the *Nephilim* terrorizing and feasting upon every living thing on the planet; no longer were the children of Cain exerting their ungodly influence upon the world scene. Theirs was a new world just waiting to be recreated in a way that could avoid all the ancient errors that had beset the previous world. If ever there was a generation with high hopes, this was it. A brand-new generation—the sons of Noah and their families—this eager bunch looked around and saw before them nothing but the potential for fulfilling the original command given to Adam and Eve, to fill the whole Earth and subdue it in the name of the Almighty.

But before long, a powerful one among the sons of Ham, his grandson by the name of Nimrod, soon turned that dream of carving out a new world on behalf of the Lord God into something altogether different. Instead of continuing to follow in the footsteps of Noah, Nimrod short-circuited the divine impulse in mankind to worship the Creator and led the people in a unifying effort to defy God in rebellion.

One can just imagine, based on what we now know about cynicism, what Nimrod might have said about the futility of following Noah in his so-called "divine unction" to repopulate Earth for the sake of the Lord God. "Noah doesn't care about you," Nimrod would have told the people. "He only cares about being your lord and master. He talks as if he speaks for God, but why would God need Noah? Let God speak for Himself! Of course if you ask me, I say God has given up on all of us. From now on, I'm all you need! The mighty hunter before the Lord! Listen to me!"

Naturally, anyone familiar with *The Bible* already knows about the Tower of Babel, but what most have never considered is how it fits into what we're interested in here. That is to say: How does this story illustrate the joy of cynicism for us? And what does it say about how the cynical mind can't resist reinterpreting the truth of our experience so that it changes something beautiful into something ugly?

The traditional view of this scenario has usually been that the rebellion of Nimrod was just another case of sinful pride, with a dash of idol worship thrown in for good measure. But in chalking up the culprit of this whodunit to pride and idols, we're no closer to ensuring that humanity will ever avoid repeating this same mistake again and again. However, if we take the time to put the dynamics of this scene in the context of our recipe for cynicism, we're much better able to counteract its impact. Let me explain.

To begin with, take a moment to recall some of the ingredients that contribute to a hardcore case of cynicism, as opposed to a healthy form of suspicion. First, there's that easy kind of skepticism that remains unchecked even in the face of evidence to the contrary. And second, there's an attitude that focuses more on God's presumed apathy and callousness and less on one's own shortcomings and failures. Then add to the mix, recall the importance of maintaining a proper sense of proportion when confronting any situation that seems too good to be true.

That said, try to imagine how you might have acted had you been among those who grew up hearing stories from your grandparents of what it was like surviving the Great Flood and being considered worthy of the awesome task of repopulating the Earth. Imagine how you might have reacted to stories in which you were being told about all that you'd one day accomplish with the help of the God of Noah. Only when we put flesh-and-blood on this scene can we ever begin to see what could have motivated the builders of that tower.

Add to those stories how intimately God interacted with Noah and his family before the Flood and then compare that with how differently God interacted with them after the Flood. This of course is another aspect of the biblical narrative that is so often overlooked when trying to understand the history of God's people. Remember our earlier discussion about the progressive nature of God's contracts that inevitably alter how God interacts with humans. Remember how God related to Adam before the Fall and how everything changed after the Fall. One can only imagine, then, how God would have similarly changed the way He interacted with Noah and his family after the judgment of the Flood.

This is critically important if we're to understand how these ingredients of cynicism blend together to create an even more potent effect had they not been so combined. In other words, while the sons of Noah were doubtlessly regaled with fantastic tales of their potential to be instruments of God in the new world, they were just as doubtlessly discouraged as they daily compared those fantastic tales with the mundane, tedious nature of the post-Flood world around them.

Then, along came a charismatic leader like Nimrod who fed their hunger in a tangible way, with a building project like nothing they could have ever conceived on their own. Again, consider Nimrod's prospects of recruiting the necessary manpower apart from the context of the recipe for cynicism. Not just because of pride or idols, mind you, but hardcore cynicism. Without men full of unbridled ambition, there's no motivation to build a tower of that magnitude. And without men whose hope of fulfilling such ambitions as, say, world conquest, there's no motivation, either. But together, they make for the perfect workforce for someone like Nimrod, just as the same ingredients have enticed ambitious men down through the long corridors of time.

Just think of all the armies of men throughout the ages who have succumbed to the same form of persuasion: men who, from their youth, are similarly told they're destined for greatness, men who are similarly foiled in fulfilling that destiny—until such a one cunningly taps into the cynicism that arises because of hope disappointed.

Then, consider the futility of any opposing view that tried to dissuade Nimrod's followers from co-operating with such a foolhardy operation. Imagine Noah and Shem trying to inspire those rebels to instead follow the better angels of their nature. Imagine them desperately urging Nimrod and his followers to not break faith with the God of the Universe. But because the Lord was no longer interacting with Noah and his family the same way as He had before the Flood, the people simply couldn't see things the way their great patriarchs saw them.

Imagine Noah and Shem's disappointment, and what they might have talked about, as they watched the tower rise, level by level, above the plains of Shinar. "My father," Shem probably said, "how can we possibly persuade our brothers to abandon this foolish and dangerous project?"

"I've been asking the Lord about the very same thing, my son," Noah would have replied. "But I freely admit, I'm at a loss. If only the Lord would respond to my prayers."

"And to think," Shem continued. "These aren't the cruel beasts of Cain who have devised this wickedness. These men sprang from the loins of the one who was to bring rest to the Earth once again."

"My sentiments exactly, my son," said Noah with a heavy sigh.

"It's as if the Heavens have become like brass," groaned Shem, "and this time God rains devastation down upon us not by a flood of water but by a flood of silence."

CHAPTER EIGHT

The Silence of God

(Because the Voice of Creation Speaks as Loudly as Any Biblical Book Ever Written)

> **INADMISSIBLE,** *an adjective*
> "Not competent to be considered... That the Scriptures are the word of God we have only the testimony of men long dead whose identity is not clearly established... Under the rules of evidence in this country, no single assertion in the Bible has in its support any evidence admissible in a court of law."
>
> *The Cynic's Word Book,* Ambrose Bierce

ONE OF THE most important things to know about the history of God's revelation is that in every age God begins by providing the highest level of His wisdom to humanity. But inevitably that wisdom is taken for granted and in response to human apathy, God withdraws His wisdom, which is then lost for an extended period, in direct relation to the length that His wisdom was present among the people of that age. Then, after a similarly extended, but very specific, period, God sparks an awakening, at which time a new generation is given another chance to appreciate what was previously squandered.

In fact, the central drama of *The Bible* is that of an infinite God Who repeatedly stoops down to interact with finite humans, how those humans respond in awe and reverence with this divine interaction, and how that marvelous relationship is inevitably spoiled by our presumption, pride, and selfishness.

It happened in the case of Adam and Eve, when God promised them eternal life, but they chose death. It happened with Noah and his children after the Great Flood, when God promised to renew the Earth, but they gathered around a tower in rebellion. And it happened to the sons of Jacob, when God called them to be a blessing to the whole world, but jealousy drove them to sell their own brother Joseph into slavery. It happened when Moses led the Children of Israel out of Egyptian bondage, but the people preferred to worship a golden calf. It happened when Joshua led the Israelites in their occupation of the Promised Land, but they chose to serve the idols of the very people they were ordered to displace. It happened when a mighty nation was forged by the hand of David and Solomon, but was later divided, just like the heart of their king who loved many strange women. And it happened when Ezra and Nehemiah inspired the Jews to rebuild the Temple at Jerusalem after their return from Babylonian Captivity, but they embraced doubt and fear when their hope in that new day faded too soon.

Considering the purpose of *The Bible* is to reveal God's ways, you'd think that anyone reading it through the ages would pick up on this pattern and resist repeating this same tendency. But sadly, mere mortals that we are, we don't. As it is written:

> There came a man who was sent from God. His name was John. He came as a witness to testify about the Light so that through him everyone might believe. He himself wasn't the Light, but he came to

testify about the Light.

The true Light Who gives light to every man was coming into the world. He was in the world, and though the world was made through Him, the world didn't recognize Him. He came to His own, and His own received Him not.

The Gospel of John

In all of this we see an emerging pattern—from Adam to Noah, from Jacob's sons to the Children of Israel, from the Jews in Ezra's day to those in Jesus' day. Again and again, God willingly communes with humanity, and they, in turn, ruin God's original plan by repeatedly turning it into something altogether alien.

Fortunately for our sake, though, the next most important thing to know about the history of God's revelation is that even when God withdraws His wisdom, in response to humanity's apathy and disregard for Him, God never entirely removes His revelation. Even though the direct revelation of God to humans is put on a "temporary hold," as it were, another form of revelation never stops communicating the knowledge of God's presence and power to an onlooking world. That other revelation is the one that is conveyed via the creation of the Universe.

This is critically important because when discussing the implications of cynicism, we admit that, in the final analysis, any point of theology may be disproved, but what can never be disproved is the self-evident reality of the creation itself. In short, you can debate all you want about the true nature of what you see around you; debate about what causes the Sun to rise, or why the sky is blue, or what makes bodies fall instead of rise. You can debate which came first: the chicken or the egg. Or debate the origins and the mystery of life. However, what you can never debate is that you exist and that the world around you exists—a life and a world filled with vitality, beauty, and grandeur. And no matter how many theological doctrines the cynic can rightly or wrongly dismiss away, the cynic can never dismiss away life itself and the creation.

This is why the Scriptures make a clear distinction between the revelation transmitted via the written word and the revelation transmitted via the creation. Said the Apostle Paul:

> They know the truth about God, as He's made it evident to them, because ever since the world was created, people have seen the Earth and sky. By way of everything that God has made, they can clearly see His invisible qualities, His eternal power, and divine nature, so they have no excuse for not knowing Him.
>
> *The Book of Romans*

Never is humanity said to be without excuse when they disagree with the testimony of Scripture. But ignore the fact that the creation itself bears witness to God's existence, quite apart from any other testimony offered by humans, and you'll find yourself suffering the consequences of your indifference. As the apostle continued to explain:

> Yes, they knew God, but they wouldn't worship Him as God or even give Him thanks, so they began to think up foolish ideas of what God was like. As a result, their minds became dark and confused. Claiming to be wise, they instead became fools.
>
> *The Book of Romans*

What is so intriguing about this statement is that the exact opposite of what we'd expect to happen ends up happening. After all, most everyone would agree that a written testimony of God's will is more articulate and therefore more understandable than the visual testimony of the creation. But if that's true, then why would God judge us more harshly when we disregard His revelation via the creation and less harshly when we disregard His revelation via the written word?

Could it be because it's easier to dismiss a written testimony, although it's presented in the name of the Lord, than it is to dismiss the physical creation as the work of Almighty God? In other words, it's easy to convince yourself that a given document is a forgery, even if the message contained in that document claims that God exists and that He has a plan for the recipients of that document. Just demonstrate that said document contains a contradiction or that it contradicts some other text that is itself considered sacred, and just that quickly, you've discredited it. In contrast to this simple exercise, it's impossible to do the same thing when analyzing the physical processes displayed in nature.

In saying this, I'm not suggesting that documents claimed to be inspired by God are dismissed as easily as detecting a contradiction here or there. As noted earlier, contradictions in biblical works aren't proof of their inauthenticity any more than when secular works are found to contain them. What I am saying is that they're simply easier to dismiss and so have less impact on one's psyche should we convince ourselves that a certain document is a forgery. This apparently is far different from when humanity encounters the works of God in the creation and then suppresses the realization that it couldn't possibly exist without the Creator's hand that set it all into motion.

Now at this point, we should address the belief in evolution as being a form of dismissing away the divine dimension of the creation and therefore the God of creation. But I'd suggest that comparing the modern dismissal of the Divine in creation with the ancient dismissal constitutes a huge error in logic. That's because when the ancients tried to eliminate the God of *The Bible* from the equation, they never once considered the creation in the same terms as their modern counterparts. In days gone by, the ancients simply turned the singular God of Creation, as described by the patriarchs and prophets, into a pantheon of lesser gods who instead animated the creation.

In contrast to that worldview, the modern-day version, which has culminated in what we now know as evolution, is such that the observed laws of nature have eliminated the need of—in their view, at least—any divine intervention. What is left is a godless Universe—in contrast to the god-filled Universe of the ancients—that is so well-regulated that it requires no need of the Divine to keep it running—again, in their view, at least.

But in either case, I'd suggest, based on the psychological evidence, there is still a price to pay for such a skewed worldview. In the past, such thinking produced pantheism, while today, it produces atheism; and for such arrogance, according to Scripture, both are as much divine punishments as they are natural consequences for such shortsightedness.

SO THE PATTERN is laid out and its contours gradually emerge, in scene after scene, as it is written:

> Listen to this, Job; stop and consider God's wonders. Do you know how God controls the clouds and makes His lightning flash? Do you know how the clouds hang poised, those wonders of Him Who has perfect knowledge?
>
> *The Book of Job*

We continue to ask the question, then: How is it possible to demonstrate that an imperfect world like ours can still be considered the product of a perfect God? Who do we believe concerning the true nature of this world and of humanity? Because our existence is filled with equal parts pain and pleasure, sadness and joy, darkness and light, death and life, should we admit that all the hardcore cynics in every age are right?

Consider the verdict of one of the most influential philosophers of the nineteenth century, John Stuart Mill, who went to great lengths to combine the best of eighteenth-century Enlightenment thinking with that of nineteenth-century Romantic and natural philosophy. A lifelong religious skeptic, Mill rejected the idea that the human mind had been given to us by God to comprehend the nature of the world. Mill insisted the human mind is simply a by-product of nature itself, and concerning the biblical concept that there is a genuine connection between the construct of the mind and the world, he stated:

> Such an inference would only be warranted if we could know *a priori* that we must have been created capable of conceiving whatever is capable of existing: that the Universe of thought and that of reality ... must have been framed in complete correspondence with one another... But an assumption more destitute of evidence could scarcely be made.
>
> *An Examination of Sir William Hamilton's Philosophy*

Based on such thinking, we'd no doubt conclude that Mill would never speculate on a topic for which he wasn't qualified by his own admission. As such, we'd naturally assume that he'd confine his remarks to the realm of the merely human, yet in violation of his own self-avowed principles, he often ventured full bore into the realm of pure speculation on the subject of God and the natural world.

But again, I say, what else would we expect? We're only human, right?

So, whether in days long ago, when Job's friends let their prejudices get the best of them, or in more recent times, when Mill offered his pat remarks, the pernicious nature of cynicism makes it very difficult to receive many a message in the same spirit in which it's given. When Job insisted that his innocence should have been obvious to all, his friends saw only his physical suffering. And with no one willing to plead his case, Job was forced, like Noah and Shem before him, to endure living in a world filled with divine silence. With no apparent word from God to directly counter his friends' accusations, Job said:

> I'm a laughingstock to my friends, though I called on God, and He answered. The righteous and upright man is a laughingstock.
>
> The one at ease scorns misfortune as the fate of those whose feet are slipping. The tents of robbers are safe, and those who provoke God are secure—those whose god is in their fists.
>
> But ask the animals, and they'll instruct you; ask the birds of the air, and they'll tell you. Or speak to the Earth, and it will teach you; let the fish of the sea inform you.
>
> Which of all these doesn't know that the hand of the Lord has done this? For the life of every living thing is in His hand, as well as the breath of all mankind.
>
> *The Book of Job*

Consider Job's response here for a moment. In naturalistic terms, it seems like the ravings of a lunatic. Clearly, Job is at his wits' end. By any normal reckoning, his logic seems out the window. But just as clearly, if you or I were in the same predicament, I'm sure we'd be just as disappointed in God's aloofness and our friends' attack. Only when we as believers consider the unique ability of Scripture to reveal things in terms that transcend our natural understanding can we begin to appreciate his response. Only then can we begin to arm ourselves against the criticisms of well-intentioned philosophers like John Stuart Mill who had a great deal to say about such things. Can you imagine his response to reading this scene from *The Bible*?

No doubt Mill could sympathize with Job regarding God's apparent unconcern for him. No doubt he'd have counseled Job to give up hoping that God would intervene any time soon. "And as for asking animals to provide you with instruction," Mill might have said to Job, "I have no idea where that's coming from. Birds of the air? Fish of the sea? Clearly you're on the verge of a nervous breakdown, my good man. Get hold of yourself. Ask the Earth to teach you? What in Heaven's name are you going on about?" For Mill, nature was thoroughly impersonal and was defined entirely by abstract laws. As he wrote:

> Since the phenomena which a thing exhibits ... are always the same in the same circumstances, they ... are called the *laws* of the thing's nature. Thus, it is a law of the nature of water that under the mean pressure of the atmosphere at the level of the sea, it boils at 212 degrees Fahrenheit...
>
> Nature means the sum of all phenomena, together with the causes which produce them; including not only all that happens, but all that can happen; the unused capabilities of causes being as much a part of the idea of Nature as those which take effect. Since all phenomena which have been sufficiently examined are found to take place with regularity ... mankind has been able to ascertain ...

the conditions of the occurrence of many phenomena; and the progress of science mainly consists in ascertaining those conditions.

When discovered, they can be expressed in general propositions, which are called ... Laws of Nature.

The Idea of God in Nature

Here we see Mill at his most restrained, which means he was describing nature in terms that he himself proscribed, such as refraining from making any unwarranted inferences. Notice however that, in describing his view of nature, he inserted a very interesting add-on. In speaking of the "sum of all phenomena," he also explained this is "including not only all that happens, but all that can happen; the unused capabilities of causes being as much a part of the idea of Nature as those which take effect." I'll have more to say about this add-on in a bit; but suffice it for now, Mill had more to write about Nature.

More importantly, what Mill wrote has much to say about how the cynical mind colors one's worldview. Because even though he usually refrained from unwarranted inferences, there's just something about discussing religious matters that undermines the best intentions of even the most disciplined philosophers. If you'll recall Mill's likely response to Job's admonition to "ask the Earth and animals to teach us," we'd hardly believe it if Mill ever suggested something so illogical. Yet despite the biblical declaration that God created the natural world for the good of mankind, Mill insisted:

> No one, either religious or irreligious, believes that the hurtful agencies of nature, considered as a whole, promote good purposes in any other way than by inciting human rational creatures to rise up

and struggle against them.

If we believed that those agencies were appointed by a benevolent Providence as the means of accomplishing wise purposes which could not be accomplished if they did not exist, then everything done by mankind which tends to chain up these natural agencies or to restrict their mischievous operation, from draining a pestilential marsh down to curing the toothache, or putting up an umbrella, ought to be accounted impious; which assuredly nobody does account them...

Inasmuch too as each generation greatly surpasses its predecessors in the amount of natural evil which it succeeds in averting, our condition, if the theory were true, ought by this time to have become a terrible manifestation of some tremendous calamity, against which the physical evils we have learned to master, had previously operated as a preservative. Anyone, however, who acted as if he supposed this to be the case, would be more likely, I think, to be confined as a lunatic than revered as a saint.

The Idea of God in Nature

Never mind that the natural world is filled with beauty beyond belief, as most people will admit, despite all that is negative and hurtful about the creation as a result of the Fall of Man. Never mind that no matter how discouraging and depressing that the stain of suffering, disease, and death is, there is still all that makes life on Earth something to be cherished.

Yet flying in the face of all that, Mill, the cynic, couldn't resist denying, in the most degrading way, any possibility that God—or Providence, as he called Him—could ever transcend such a miserable state of affairs. And this, Mill stated, despite his own insistence that within "the sum of all phenomena," which is Nature, there is still always the possibility of something happening that hasn't happened yet. And it was this that Mill described as "the unused capabilities of causes being as much a part of the idea of Nature as those which take effect."

JUST AS the debate between Job and his friends, about the moral foundations by which to judge God, conveys a universal paradigm, so does Mill's cynicism of the current state of the world regarding its apparent imperfections. While many people lean toward agnosticism and atheism if they consider the injustices in life are inconsistent with a loving or just God, we see a similar response when looking at the bittersweet dynamics of the natural world, especially in regard to the animal kingdom, characterized by what Heinrich Ewald called "the destiny of severe suffering and pain," in which:

> The violent live the most securely, as the vulture lives more securely than the dove, the lion than the ox, the shark than the dolphin, the rose than the thorn which tears it.
>
> *Jamieson-Fausset-Brown Bible Commentary*

In examining this complex issue, I'd suggest that we approach it from several angles in the hopes of avoiding a biased worldview. So far we have Job and his friends from days gone by, and from more recent times, we have John Stuart Mill. Now I'd like to introduce another set of contributors: First, we'll hear from the eighteenth-century Scottish Enlightenment philosopher David Hume, and then from several other esteemed commentators.

We proceed next with Hume, because in looking to maintain an unbiased approach to Nature, it's critical that we answer the objection of anyone who insists it's only natural for Mill to be cynical about the idea of God in Nature because that was the predominant worldview of that time period.

To some extent, there are similarities in both men's thinking, although not in every respect, as we'll soon see. Like Mill, David Hume was well-known for his religious skepticism. Speaking on the typical approach to religious thought, Hume wrote:

> If we take in our hand any volume—of divinity or school metaphysics, for instance—let us ask: Does it contain any abstract reasoning about quantity or number? No. Does it contain any experiential reasoning about matters of fact and existence? No. Then throw it in the fire, for it can contain nothing but sophistry and illusion.
>
> *An Inquiry Concerning Human Understanding*

Hume was once deprived of a teaching position at the University of Edinburgh because he was seen as an atheist; and his religious views were so suspicious that his friends had to intervene on his behalf so that he could avoid being tried for heresy. Clearly, then, Hume—again, like Mill—could never be confused with your typical Bible-believing Christian. Yet when it came to the idea of God in Nature, the two men couldn't have seen things more differently.

While Mill saw only "mischievous operations, natural evils, and tremendous calamities," with which humans were forced to endure, Hume saw past such defects in Nature. As he wrote concerning the evidence of a Creator by way of the element of design in the creation:

> Suppose that there is a natural, universal, invariable language, common to every individual of the human race; and that books are natural products

which perpetuate themselves in the same way as animals and plants do, by descent and propagation. These suppositions aren't as wildly far from fact as you might think. We do have a kind of universal language, embedded in some expressions of our passions; and all the lower animals have a natural speech, which, however limited, is very intelligible to their own species. And as the finest and most eloquent text is infinitely less complex and intricate than the coarsest organism, the propagation of an *Iliad* or *Aeneid* is easier to suppose than that of any plant or animal.

So choose sides, without ambiguity or evasion; either assert that a book needn't have a rational cause, or admit a similar cause for all the works of Nature.

Dialogues Concerning Natural Religion

Hume's argument here was like many other great thinkers throughout history who saw the connection between the design in natural objects and their creators as being analogous with the connection between the design in Nature and the Great Creator. Said the ancient Roman statesman Cicero:

When you look at a picture or a statue, you recognize it is a work of art. When you follow from afar the course of a ship on the sea, you don't question that its movement is guided by a skilled intelligence. When you see a sundial or a water-clock, you see it tells the time by design and not by chance. How then can you imagine that the Universe as a whole is devoid of purpose and intelligence, when it embraces everything, including these creations themselves and their creators?

> Our friend Posidonius as you know has recently made a globe which in its revolution shows the movements of the Sun and stars and planets, by day and night, just as they appear in the sky. Now if someone were to take this globe and show it to the people of Britain or Scythia would a single one of those barbarians fail to see that it was the product of a conscious intelligence?
>
> *On the Nature of the Gods*

Similarly, the seventeenth-century English physicist Isaac Newton said, "the regular motion of the planets make it reasonable to believe in the continued existence of God," and French philosopher Rene Descartes said, "the cosmos is a great time machine operating according to fixed laws, a watch created and wound up by the great watchmaker." Then there was the eighteenth-century English theologian David Butler who said:

> As the manifold appearances of design and of final causes, in the constitution of the world, prove it to be the work of an intelligent Mind... The appearances of *design* and of *final Causes* in the constitution of Nature ... prove this acting agent to be an *intelligent Designer...* Ten thousand instances of design cannot but prove a Designer.
>
> *The Analogy of Religion, Natural and Revealed, to the Constitution and Course of Nature*

Then there was the Genevan philosopher Jean-Jacques Rousseau who added to this idea of the divine watchmaker. (Incidentally, just as important are his remarks that correlate with the question we're concerned with here: How do we reconcile this imperfect world as being the product of a perfect God? Because although humans can recognize the Creator's hand in Nature's design, we're still left wrestling with the pain and suffering experienced not just by us but by all living creatures on this planet. In the opening line to Rousseau's book, he stated: "Everything is good as it leaves the hands of the Author of things; everything degenerates in the hands of man.") From there, despite his admittedly pessimistic view of mankind, Rousseau proceeded to ponder the idea of design in Nature:

> I am like a man who sees the works of a watch for the first time; he is never weary of admiring the mechanism, though he does not know the use of the instrument and has never seen its face. I do not know what this is for, says he, but I see that each part of it is fitted to the rest, I admire the workman in the details of his work, and I am quite certain that all these wheels only work together in this fashion for some common end which I cannot perceive.
>
> Let us compare the special ends, the means, the ordered relations of every kind, then let us listen to the inner voice of feeling; what healthy mind can reject its evidence? Unless the eyes are blinded by prejudices, can they fail to see that the visible order of the Universe proclaims a supreme intelligence? What sophisms must be brought together before we fail to understand the harmony of existence and the wonderful co-operation of every part for the maintenance of the rest?
>
> *Emile, or Treatise on Education*

Especially important to our train of thought, David Hume also weighed in on the idea of the workings of the Universe as indicating that a Creator is behind it all:

> Look around the world, contemplating the whole thing and every part of it; you'll find that it is nothing but one big machine subdivided into an infinite number of smaller ones, which in their turn could be subdivided to a degree beyond what human senses and faculties can trace and explain. All these various machines, and even their most minute parts, are adjusted to each other so precisely that everyone who has ever contemplated them is filled with wonder. The intricate fitting of means to ends throughout all nature is just like (though more wonderful than) the fitting of means to ends in things that have been produced by us—products of human designs, thought, wisdom, and intelligence. Since the effects resemble each other, we are led to infer by all the rules of analogy that the causes are also alike, and that the author of nature is somewhat similar to the mind of man, though he has much larger faculties to go with the grandeur of the work he has carried out. By this argument *a posteriori*, and by this argument alone, do we prove both that there is a God and that He resembles human mind and intelligence.
>
> *Dialogues Concerning Natural Religion*

And finally, there is perhaps the most important expression of the idea of the creation as a great clock in the hands of God, the Great Clockmaker. In his 1802 book, the nineteenth-century English philosopher William Paley sparked a revolution, when he wrote in his preface:

> In crossing a heath, suppose I pitched my foot against a stone, and were asked how the stone came to be there; I might possibly answer, that, for anything I knew to the contrary, it had lain there for-

ever: nor would it perhaps be very easy to show the absurdity of this answer. But suppose I had found a watch upon the ground, and it should be inquired how the watch happened to be in that place; I should hardly think of the answer I had before given, that for anything I knew, the watch might have always been there... There must have existed, at some time, and at some place, a creator or creators, who formed (the watch) for the purpose which we find it ... who comprehended its construction, and designed its use... Every indication of contrivance, every manifestation of design, which existed in the watch, exists in the works of nature; with the difference, on the side of nature, of being greater, and that in a degree which exceeds all computation.

Natural Theology, or Evidences of the Existence and Attributes of the Deity

In all these thoughtful explanations, we see the apostle's words perfectly illustrated regarding the revelatory function of the natural world. Quite apart from God's revelation in scriptural form, then, the voice of creation speaks as loudly as any biblical book ever written. Keith Thomson sums up this idea perfectly when he writes:

One of the great assets of natural theology, and the evidence it drew from the world of the living animals and plants, is that it was understandable to a broad following who did not have to know code words of contemporary philosophy, or have mastered calculus or chemistry to follow the argument completely. Natural history enjoys a privileged position among the sciences both in its broad accessibility and in the extraordinary aesthetic pleasure inherent in the subject. This is obvious to amateur and professional alike, and only increases the more deeply one probes into the complexities of life. One has only to think of the mechanical precision underlying the flowing grace of a cheetah in full stride or the whorled mathematical precision of a sunflower...

Such glories of nature have always been the principal evidence that natural theologians adduce for the existence of a creating God—the argument *a posteriori* that Hume allowed as the only possible proof. The vast bulk of writing in natural theology is taken up with elucidating and sermonizing upon long lists of such examples from nature; they are the basic evidence for the prosecution's case: such perfections of design and function appear to require us to conclude that a master creator has been at work.

Before Darwin: Reconciling God and Nature

The only thing I find more intriguing than that so many of the greatest minds of the West have all tuned into this truth is that except for a few like Paley, most still had a hard time believing the same Deity they identified as the Creator would choose to reveal Himself in the pages of *The Bible*.

CHAPTER NINE

The Economy of Nature
(Because God Always Knew How to Transcend the Power of Death)

> **EDIBLE,** *an adjective*
> "Good to eat and wholesome to digest, as a worm to a toad, a toad to a snake, a snake to a pig, a pig to a man, and a man to a worm."
>
> *The Cynic's Word Book,* Ambrose Bierce

NOW THAT we've established how the creation itself serves as a divinely inspired form of communication, let's look at the various ways humans interpret that information, and how that in turn shapes our worldview and thus shapes the world we live in.

So far, we've generally thought of this idea of interpretation as something that creates atheists out of those who reject God's existence and theists out of those who accept that He exists. We've also pointed out that this rejection of God doesn't happen so much because of what most assume prevents atheists from believing in God or accepting the truth of *The Bible*. Here I'm suggesting that the real enemy of these things is cynicism.

When confronted by the truth as God presents it, whether through the articulate word of His human messengers or the inarticulate word of the creation's voice, cynics can't resist reinterpreting that message so it "falls on deaf ears," as it were. What's more, because cynics insist on deciding if there is a God based on the perceived goodness—or lack thereof—of those who profess to be followers of this God, they can't help but dismiss a God Who would be responsible for such hypocritical behavior. Add to that the contradictory aspects of the biblical message that flow from an undisciplined study of Scripture, which is inherently steeped in the paradoxical nature of truth, and one can easily understand why such cynicism leads someone into agnosticism or atheism.

In a situation like this, we naturally assume that cynicism creates a dividing line between believers and unbelievers, between theists and atheists. But in looking at how *The Bible* speaks of Nature's role in communicating God's word to humanity something quite unexpected comes to light. We see that cynicism not only undermines the ability of agnostics and atheists to appreciate the authenticity of Scripture, but it also does the same thing for a vast portion of those who claim to believe in God as the Creator of the Universe.

That's because the great irony in some people's ability to see God via the design factor in Nature is how it spawns two distinct ways of thinking in so-called "believers." The first group is known as theists; the second, deists. By definition, a theist is someone who believes in the existence of God, especially One Who created the world and Who acts to influence events, whereas a deist is someone who believes in a God Who created the world but Who doesn't act to influence events. At one end of the spectrum, theism states that the existence and continuance of the Universe is owed to a Supreme Being Who is distinct from the creation. For this reason, theism proclaims a dualistic relationship between God and the world, with God controlling events from beyond the human sphere. On the other end, deism states that while a Supreme Being exists and has created the Universe, He doesn't as a rule intervene in human affairs and so revelation as a means of divine communication is rejected.

This means that when it comes to the design factor in Nature, theists take this as simply a starting point in their search for revelatory knowledge as it's found in Scripture. As such, for the theist, the creation provides the necessary proof that supports the next logical step for them, which is that God also speaks directly to humanity. On the other hand, deists insist that the physical evidence obtained from the observation of Nature is all that is necessary in one's search for truth. As such, for the deist, any discussion of the supernatural in *The Bible*, especially when it comes to talk of revelation or miracles, is wholly unnecessary in one's pursuit of divine wisdom.

One such deist who rejected any need of the supernatural from God was the eighteenth-century English-born American political activist Thomas Paine, who insisted:

> But when the divine gift of reason begins to expand itself in the mind and calls man to reflection, he then reads and contemplates God and His works, and not in the books pretending to be revelation. The creation is *The Bible* of the true believer in God. Everything in this vast volume inspires him with sublime ideas of the Creator. The little and paltry, and often obscene, tales of *The Bible* sink into wretchedness when put in comparison with this mighty work.
>
> The Deist needs none of those tricks and shows called miracles to confirm his faith, for what can be a greater miracle than the creation itself, and His

own existence?

There is a happiness in Deism, when rightly understood, that is not to be found in any other system of religion. All other systems have something in them that either shock our reason, or are repugnant to it, and man, if he thinks at all, must stifle his reason in order to force himself to believe them.

But in Deism our reason and our belief become happily united. The wonderful structure of the Universe, and everything we behold in the system of the creation, prove to us, far better than books can do, the existence of a God, and at the same time proclaim His attributes.

It is by the exercise of our reason that we are enabled to contemplate God in His works, and imitate Him in His ways. When we see His care and goodness extended over all His creatures, it teaches us our duty toward each other, while it calls forth our gratitude to Him. It is by forgetting God in His works, and running after the books of pretended revelation, that man has wandered from the straight path of duty and happiness, and become by turns the victim of doubt and the dupe of delusion.

Of the Religion of Deism Compared with the Christian Religion

A more biting and sarcastic portrayal of how differently deists and theists view *The Bible* can hardly be found. Sadly, though, while Paine's extolling of Nature as *The Bible* of the true believer seems honest enough, it does so only when Paine's remarks are seen in isolation. By that I mean, while Paine waxed eloquently on the virtues of deism as being the happiest of religions and the product of the divine gift of reason, he's really nothing more than a hardcore cynic "in deist's clothing," as it were. Which is just another way of saying that when it comes to Paine's views about the flaws of theism, he spent a lifetime focusing on what I've repeatedly described as the joy of cynicism as opposed to the struggle of faith.

As you'll recall, cynics always take the easy path of focusing on the inconsistencies in Scripture instead of the hard path of reconciling its paradoxical quality. As such, it's much easier to highlight the human tragedy in the tale, which Paine prided himself on perceiving in others, rather than face his own inability to do the hard work of reading the whole book of God and so let it speak for itself. Regarding the superiority of deism over theism, Paine wrote:

> Of all the systems of religion that ever were invented, there is none more derogatory to the Almighty, more unedifying to man, more repugnant to reason, and more contradictory in itself, than this thing called Christianity. Too absurd for belief, too impossible to convince, and too inconsistent for practice, it renders the heart torpid, or produces only atheists and fanatics. As an engine of power, it serves the purpose of despotism; and as a means of wealth, the avarice of priests; but so far as respects the good of man in general, it leads to nothing here or hereafter.
>
> The only religion that has not been invented, and that has in it every evidence of divine originality, is pure and simple deism. It must have been the first and will probably be the last that man believes. But pure and simple deism does not answer the purpose of despotic governments.
>
> They cannot lay hold of religion as an engine but by mixing it with human inventions, and making their own authority a part; neither does it answer the avarice of priests, but by incorporating them-

selves and their functions with it, and becoming, like the government, a party in the system. It is this that forms the otherwise mysterious connection of church and state; the church human, and the state tyrannic.

The Age of Reason

Admittedly, Paine was justified in his criticism of hypocritical behavior—of priestly avarice and tyrannical states, of fanatics and despots. But in truth, his scathing indictment would have been just as correct if he'd aimed his analysis on any human organization, be it religious or otherwise. As such, Paine's cause would have been better served had he tempered his view by letting us know that the corruptibility of power has never been exclusive to Christian institutions or leaders.

In the end, although Paine's views were correct to a certain degree, his praise of the revelatory aspect of Nature was overshadowed by his incorrect view that everything in Scripture is negated by the hypocrisy of said church or state. As we've already seen in a previous chapter, the problem of inconsistencies in Scripture can't negate the truth in them; the real problem, as in all cases like this, is the toxic level of cynicism that prevents men as intelligent as even Paine from looking beyond human frailty and beyond the paradoxical nature of *The Bible* to see the larger truth contained in God's written revelation.

What's more, the real tragedy for so many of the great deists of that age is that while they were correct in their healthy suspicion, in seeing through religious hypocrisy and abuse, they let their personal bias blind them from perceiving what the truth of Nature was designed to do in the first place. As you'll recall the pattern we've highlighted throughout this work: When God gives His wisdom to humanity, from age to age, that wisdom is inevitably taken for granted, and eventually followed by the withdrawal of that wisdom. It is then that the specific revelation of God gives way to the general revelation via the creation. What deists forget, then, in their misguided zeal, is that the same God Who can create the grand clock of Nature can also provide the written revelation of Scripture.

So, in comparing the worldview of the theist and the deist, we see how these divergent perspectives spawn two clear and obvious conclusions for those who contemplate the supernatural features as they're described in *The Bible*.

First, if the creation reveals tangible evidence of a Creator Who is responsible for the immensity and complexity of the Universe, then who could reject the possibility that this all-powerful being can communicate with His own creatures. In short, how absurd to think that the One Who created the mouth can't speak, or created the eyes and can't be seen, or created the ears and can't be heard. The two ideas are by any standard of logic entirely incompatible.

Second, if Nature itself reveals the pen of a supernatural Author, then how else would this marvelous creation reveal itself except in terms of this supernatural authorship, in contrast to the merely natural creatures that reside on this planet. By that I mean to say, that while humans and animals are typically known for their finite nature, the planet as a whole seems to take on a kind of infinite dimension in terms of its self-regulating, self-organizing ecosystems.

Upon analysis of the Earth's biosphere, it could be said that it is based on what would otherwise be considered miraculous processes, which is to say, within the matrix of life there is a marvelous pattern of death and rebirth. On every level of existence, from the lowest lifeforms to the most complex, there is a mysterious confluence in which each lifeform is dependent on the expiration of some other lifeform. Even in death, then, matter is never lost but is always transformed from one level of existence to another, ecologically speaking. The nineteenth-century French chemist Jean-Baptiste Dumas described it this way:

> Everything that the plants take from the air, they give to animals, then the animals return it to the air; this is the eternal circle in which life revolves but where matter only changes place.
>
> *On the Chemical Statics of Organized Beings*

That being the evidence available to us, then why hasn't anyone who supports the miraculous in Scripture ever pointed to this unique quality of Nature, and asked the obvious next questions: Is this what we'd expect from a purely naturalistic world? Couldn't the biosphere of Earth function just as efficiently if all biological lifeforms lived and procreated independently of one another? Why not, instead, have every lifeform spontaneously generate and then sustain itself without any need of the death of other organisms? When something dies, why not have it simply biodegrade into nothingness?

What's more, if this ecological cycle is no accident in terms of God's intention, then why haven't theists ever thought to leverage this "coincidence" to justify their position, if, that is, considering the magnitude of this pattern of death and rebirth, this could ever be deemed coincidental? And if so, then why not force the hand of deists to relinquish their position that the record of miracles or revelation in *The Bible* is merely a man-made contrivance only good for controlling the masses?

Just consider what we've all heard about but never think to connect. As proponents of a divine worldview, whether you consider yourself a theist or a deist: Have you ever noticed how both Nature and Scripture reveal a similar pattern in the way that death and rebirth are enacted? In Nature, we see this pattern played out in the Earth's biosphere, in which every stratum of life depends, symbiotically, upon the death of a great many others. And in Scripture, we see this pattern played out in the various occurrences of death and resurrection, whether figuratively or literally, that all foreshadow and culminate in the death and resurrection of the Word of God Himself, Jesus Christ.

Taken together, this dual pattern clearly points to a powerful conclusion: If Nature and Scripture reveal a correspondence between something so improbable as death and rebirth, then this confirms that the written record of Scripture—with all its messy talk of miracles and revelation—is simply the inevitable and thoroughly natural by-product of a supernaturally designed Universe.

IN ASKING why no one has ever connected this pattern of death and rebirth in both Nature and Scripture, the most obvious answer is that for most of history the process as it's found in the natural world went unnoticed. It wasn't until the seventeenth century, actually, that we began to connect the dots, and then only slowly did a genuine understanding begin to come to light. Describing this emerging process, the Anglo-Irish natural philosopher and chemist Robert Boyle wrote:

> The book of Nature is a fine and large piece of tapestry rolled up, which we are not able to see all at once, but must be content to wait for the discovery of its beauty and symmetry, little by little, as it gradually comes to be more and more unfolded, or displayed.
>
> *The Christian Virtuoso*

Best known for his work as one of the pioneers of the scientific method, Robert Boyle is generally regarded as the father of modern chemistry. His book *The Skeptical Chemist* is considered a cornerstone in the field of chemistry.

Concerning his many contributions to science, Edward B. Davis says:

> Few natural philosophers influenced the rise of modern science more than Robert Boyle...
>
> A superb experimentalist and diligent collector of information about many aspects of nature, Boyle did as much as anyone else to create the modern laboratory, the methods it employs, and the scientific papers it produces. His publications were read throughout Europe and in parts of North America because the subtlety and precision of his work was matched only by the range of his knowledge and the honesty and clarity of his reports. In short, Boyle showed the world how science ought to be done: we might even say that his most important discovery was the activity of science itself.
>
> *Robert Boyle, the Bible, and Natural Philosophy*

Yet as devoted as he was to pursuing scientific knowledge, Boyle was even more devoted to applying that knowledge in the pursuit of natural philosophy, which he was convinced provided tangible evidence for the existence of God. As Boyle described it:

> When with bold telescopes I survey the old and newly discovered stars and planets, when with excellent microscopes I discern the inimitable subtlety of nature's curious workmanship, and when by the help of anatomical knives and the light of chemical furnaces I study the book of Nature I often find myself reduced to exclaim with the psalmist: "How manifold are Your works, oh Lord! In wisdom You have made them all!"
>
> *Seraphic Love*

Not stopping there, though, Boyle insisted that the natural world was no passive environment but, rather, could be used to demonstrate God's active involvement in the world.

Born in the same year of 1627 as Boyle, the English clergyman and naturalist John Ray added to the development of natural philosophy, biology, botany, and zoology. From his lectures and sermons around 1660, Ray produced a book that became the first English manifesto of natural theology. In it he encouraged a common-sense approach to the matter, writing:

> You may hear illiterate persons of the lowest rank of the commonality affirming that they need no proof of the being of God, for that every pile of grass, or ear of corn sufficiently proves that. For, they say, all the men of the world cannot make such a thing as one of these; and if they cannot do it, who can or did make it but God? To tell them that it made itself, or sprang up by chance, would be as ridiculous as to tell the greatest philosophers so.
>
> *The Wisdom of God Manifested in the Works of Creation*

Ray's most significant contributions came in establishing the argument of design in Nature as a proof of God's existence, and in defining one of the foundational concepts in biology, which is to say, that of the notion of a "species," as a "group of morphologically similar organisms arising from a common ancestor."

At the same time the English natural philosopher Kenelm Digby was systematizing the processes of nature in the same way early economists did with agrarian societies of the day. By observing plants and animals in their natural habitats, Digby laid the foundation for a new system that, like Ray, was to have a lasting impact not only in the field of natural history but would one day impact another worldview that was diametrically opposed to it. More on this unexpected twist of fate later, but for now, we'll continue looking at the early stages of this critical development of natural history, or, as it came to be known, natural theology. The legacy of Digby's pioneering work was that by combining the idea of design in Nature and the economic principles of his day, he postulated a new worldview whereby every creature—both human and non-human—existed at the center of its own "economy of nature."

The seventeenth century was a pivotal period in the development of natural history. The ancient worldview of Aristotle, which had been handed down by many of the early Church Fathers, was gradually falling out of favor. As Peter C. Remien described it:

> The Aristotelian tendency to personify inanimate objects in order to explain their behavior came to be seen as a sign of incomprehensibility and absurdity...
>
> In place of the Aristotelian model, thinkers such as Galileo, Descartes, Hobbes, and Newton constructed mechanistic systems for understanding the workings of nature. In these systems, fixed laws replaced diffuse agency. Unlike the Aristotelian system, which relied upon organic metaphors, mechanism drew upon the metaphorics of technological innovations such as clocks and watches in order to conceptualize the rational workings of nature...
>
> But just as the organic metaphorics of the Aristotelians failed to explain phenomena such as the predictable motions of projectiles with the exactitude of mechanical philosophy, the new mechanical systems had trouble accommodating the choice, error, and randomness intrinsic to the study of life.

Thus Digby, in attempting to create a conceptual model of the terrestrial world capable of explaining the behavior of both living and non-living bodies, evokes the more flexible metaphorics of economy as a way of negotiating Aristotelian and mechanistic worldviews. The "economy of nature" represented a physics of life—a system capable of expressing the orderly, though sometimes unpredictable, interactions between living creatures and their environments.

> *The Oeconomy of Nature: Literature and Ecology in the English Renaissance*

And as Remien went on to explain how, for Digby:

The Economy of Nature is wedded to divine providence as the means through which God reveals His presence to humankind. Digby suggests that although our senses are too limited to comprehend the immense scope of nature, our recognition that nature works with economy allows us to infer the existence of divinity. Economy becomes a way of recognizing the order behind sublime complexity. Divinity in this conceptual scheme lies in the vanishing point within our vision of nature. It is the point at which our senses become inadequate to the task of comprehension. In other words, while we cannot possibly achieve a vision of the Economy of Nature in its entirety, its very existence implies the divine architecture of the world.

> *The Oeconomy of Nature: Literature and Ecology in the English Renaissance*

Soon, other thinkers of that era picked up on the idea of the Economy of Nature, and slowly but surely it began to resonate throughout the expanding field of natural theology. There was the English theologian and cosmologist Thomas Burnet who, in his 1691 publication, built on the idea:

> This "economy of nature," as I may call it—or well ordering of the great family of living creatures—is an argument both of goodness and of wisdom, and is in every way far above the powers of brute matter.
>
> All regular administration we ascribe to conduct and judgment: If an army of men be well provided for in things necessary for food, clothes, arms, lodging, security, and defense, so as nothing is wanting in so great a multitude, we suppose it the effect of care and forecast in those persons that had the charge of it; they took their measures at first, computed and proportioned one thing to another, made good regulations, and gave orders for convenient supplies.
>
> And can we suppose the great army of creatures upon Earth managed and provided for with less forethought and Providence, no, with none at all, by mere chance? This is to recede from all rules and analogy of reason, only to serve a turn, and gratify an unreasonable humor.
>
> *The Sacred Theory of the Earth*

In short, Burnet made the argument that nobody would ever think that a human army could be adequately supplied through some accidental means, so why would anyone think the Creator wasn't responsible for supplying humanity with its vast army of creatures without which life on Earth would be unsustainable? To Burnet the idea was not only unreasonable, it was downright laughable.

Then there is the eighteenth-century Swedish botanist

Carl Linnaeus, who is best known for *The System of Nature*, in which he established the first system of classifying the natural world into three distinct kingdoms: animal, plant, and mineral. In another of his works, Linnaeus added to the idea of the "economy of nature," where he outlined the propagation, preservation, and destruction of the plant and animal kingdoms as being the phenomena which maintained this economy.

According to Geir Hestmark, Linnaeus was "a faithful observer of nature's ways, whose acute and comprehensive first-hand experience set him apart from the previous physico-theologists, who were more philosophers than naturalists." According to Linnaeus, the natural world clearly reveals an ecosystem that:

> Revolves around the fate of the individual, the fundamental processes or stages in the life cycle: Creation/birth (*generatio*), Maintenance (*conservatio*) and finally Destruction (*destructio*)—in plants, animals and rocks. Linnaeus paints a vivid picture of how these processes create a flow of matter through nature—what we would refer to as the great biogeochemical cycles—so that everything is connected and nothing is really lost. And although individuals perish, their roles persist.
>
> *Oeconomia Naturae L.*

As Hestmark described it further:

> *The Economy of Nature* is both the culmination of a great tradition ... of Christian natural theology, and the starting point of a new science, the one that Ernst Haeckel named "ecology" in 1866. In accordance with the natural theology and the "age of optimism" ... Linnaeus defines "the economy of nature"

as the Creator's wise arrangement and deposition of all things according to which they fulfill their purpose for the glory of God and the happiness of man.

Oeconomia Naturae L.

Like many of his learned predecessors, Linnaeus wasn't just a man of science; he was also a man of faith. Convinced that God had led him into his study of the natural world, he explained in his 1749 book:

> To perpetuate the established course of Nature in a continued series, the divine wisdom has thought fit, that all living creatures should constantly be employed in producing individuals, that all natural things should contribute and lend a helping hand towards preserving every species, and lastly that the death and destruction of one thing should always be subservient to the restitution of another.

The Economy of Nature

Such a conception of the natural world, one which posits that natural things could "contribute and lend a helping hand towards preserving every species" (including humans) is, of course, something that no deist could ever endure. For men like Mill, Hume, and Paine the natural world may have been created by God, it may have been set into motion by God, but in the opinion of the diehard deist, that was where God's involvement ended. To believe otherwise, would have dragged all of them into territory where they adamantly refused to go. If they could ever be convinced that God did more than create and vacate, then they'd be forced to rethink their entire perspective on all those other messy areas regarding the miraculous and revelatory.

But all one has to do is recall Mill's potential response to Job's situation, in which Job is told to look to the animals and the Earth to gain divine insight into his own suffering, and it comes as no surprise when we confront what Mill said concerning the idea of God in Nature:

> If there are any marks at all of special design in creation, one of the things most evidently designed is that a large proportion of all animals should pass their existence in tormenting and devouring other animals. They have been lavishly fitted out with the instruments necessary for that purpose; their strongest instincts impel them to it, and many of them seem to have been constructed incapable of supporting themselves by any other food.
>
> If a tenth part of the pains which have been expended in finding benevolent adaptations in all nature had been employed in collecting evidence to blacken the character of the Creator, what scope for comment would not have been found in the entire existence of the lower animals, divided with scarcely an exception, into devourers and devoured, and a prey to a thousand ills from which they are denied the faculties necessary for protecting themselves!
>
> If we are not obliged to believe the animal creation to be the work of a demon, it is because we need not suppose it to have been made by a Being of infinite power. But if imitation of the Creator's will, as is revealed in nature, were applied as a rule of action in this case, the most atrocious enormities of the worst men would be more than justified by the apparent intention of Providence that throughout all animated nature the strong should prey upon the weak.
>
> *The Idea of God in Nature*

Like Paine before him, in his damning indictment of corrupt theists, Mill levels an egregious blow to the integrity of the Creator Who in his view is acting more like a demon than an angel in His organization of the natural world. In rebuttal, several things need to be introduced if we're to "right the ship," so to speak.

The first thing is to face the fact that *The Bible* never tries to sugar-coat this tragic aspect of the creation, which is clearly not the result of a choice originally instituted at the beginning of His created world. When God completed the creation, it was said that it was good and as such anyone who has heard this before can't help but acknowledge that this was said prior to the Fall of Man, and prior to the time that death entered the world. As you'll recall the words of Rousseau, who said, "Everything is good as it leaves the hands of the Author of things; everything degenerates in the hands of man."

This is confirmed in the biblical record that states, in no uncertain terms, God didn't choose death for humanity; Adam and Eve did. But of course, we now know that the real issue isn't our all-too-tragic experience of suffering, disease, and death, because of what we already addressed: Even though death wasn't necessarily the only outcome of unleashing freedom into the world, God always knew how to transcend such an outcome and even use this to fulfill a higher purpose. Still, this was an idea that Mill, for all his genius in every other arena of life, refused to entertain. Again, recall how he railed:

> If we believed that those agencies were appointed by a benevolent Providence as the means of accomplishing wise purposes which could not be accomplished if they did not exist, then everything done by mankind which tends to chain up these natural agencies or to restrict their mischievous operation,

from draining a pestilential marsh down to curing the toothache, or putting up an umbrella, ought to be accounted impious; which assuredly nobody does account them.

The Idea of God in Nature

Notwithstanding Mill's objection, this is what God has done: He allowed death to enter the world, and in a completely unexpected way, He turned it inside out so we could, as previously stated, partake of the dualities of life without which there'd be no potential for faith, hope, and love.

The only thing that remains, then, is to demonstrate how God accomplished this astonishing reversal of the tragedy of death that was turned instead into the miracle of life. And more importantly, we need to examine how God is doing this so that it survives that other great enemy of life: cynicism. Because even if one were to adequately explain how God has worked out this miracle—not merely in philosophical terms but in actual concrete ones—there is still the risk that this explanation will simply be reinterpreted to mean something else.

CHAPTER TEN

From Economy to Ecology
(Because Death is the Only Means to the Renewal of Life)

> **EMBALM,** *a verb*
> To cheat vegetation by locking up the gases upon which it feeds. By embalming their dead and thereby deranging the natural balance between animal and vegetable life, the Egyptians made their once fertile and populous country barren and incapable of supporting more than a meager crew. The modern metallic burial casket is a step in the same direction, and many a dead man who ought now to be ornamenting his neighbor's lawn as a tree, or enriching his table as a bunch of radishes, is doomed to a long inutility.
>
> *The Cynic's Word Book,* Ambrose Bierce

FOR MOST people, the biblical worldview has typically seen death in negative terms. Death entered the world as the result of Adam and Eve's disobedience. Following that, *The Bible* depicts the death of wrongdoers as punishment for their misdeeds, from Noah's Deluge to the destruction of Sodom and Gomorrah. Even though Jesus knew He was about to raise His friend from the grave, He still wept when Lazarus died. And in Paul's first letter to the Corinthians, he stated that "the last enemy to be destroyed will be death."

Seen in that context alone, then, it may surprise most people when first confronted with what I stated earlier, about how we could never know what it means to be truly human had we never been subjected to suffering, disease, and death. That's because while death is clearly a dreaded enemy on a personal level, we have to admit, when seen through the lens of the overall biblical message, there's more than meets the eye, as with all the deepest truths of Scripture, even when that message involves death. After all, if this weren't true, then how are we to understand the words of the psalmist, who wrote, "The death of His saints is precious in the sight of the Lord."

Be that as it may, there is still great irony in the possibility that death has just as much potential for good as it has for bad. That's because while Christians might profess to this belief as a point of theology, many of us—myself included—still have a very difficult time reconciling points of doctrine with points of real life when it comes to personally coming to grips with death. The irony I'm speaking of consists of the following disconnected kind of thinking: Many of us may profess to believe in the Scriptures, but when punched in the gut by the death of a loved one, we rarely in that instant recall biblical messages of hope in such times of crisis.

Recall what Paul also said to the Corinthians, in that being "absent from the body" is to be "with the Lord." In this he was certainly thinking of something else that the psalmist said: "But God will redeem my life from the grave; He will certainly take me to Himself." So from *The Old Testament* to *The New Testament*, the same theme echoes throughout:

> For this God is our God for ever and ever: He will be our guide even to the point of death.
>
> *The Book of Psalms*

> He will swallow up death forever. Then the Lord God will wipe away the tears from all faces.
>
> *The Book of Isaiah*

> I will ransom them from the power of the grave; I'll redeem them from death. Where, oh death, are your plagues? Where, oh grave, is your destruction?
>
> *The Book of Hosea*

> For since death came through a man, the resurrection of the dead comes also through a man. For as in Adam all die, so in Christ all will be made alive…
>
> So it will be with the resurrection of the dead. The body that is sown is perishable, it is raised imperishable; it is sown in dishonor, it is raised in glory; it is sown in weakness, it is raised in power; it is sown a natural body, it is raised a spiritual body.
>
> *The First Book of Corinthians*

> Jesus said, "I am the Resurrection and the Life. Those who believe in Me, even though they die, will live, and everyone who lives and believes in Me will never die."
>
> *The Gospel of John*

Now in speaking of the irony in looking to such passages, I'd like to challenge you with the following: How do you characterize yourself? Are you a theist who believes in Scripture as the main form of God's communication, but because Nature is merely the product of the Divine it contributes little in the way of revelation? Or are you a deist who believes in Nature alone as God's revelatory instrument but sees no value in the so-called "written revelation" because it's the product of mere mortals? Or are you an atheist who believes that neither Nature nor Scripture can provide divine revelation because Nature is the product of random, impersonal forces, and Scripture, the product of finite, fallible persons?

The irony I'm thinking of, then, lies in the fact that without fully appreciating the role that Nature plays, all three of these worldviews are deficient in the very thing each group insists is important and true about the world. What do I mean by that? Well, let me take some time to explain, and in doing so, weave together everything that we've gathered so far in asking the same question we asked when we first began our investigation. And as usual, we'll pay particular attention to the role that cynicism plays in coloring one's response to any answers to this question.

THE QUESTION, as you'll recall, is: How can we sincerely believe that the imperfect world we live in was created by a perfect God? Let's begin by establishing, with as much impartiality as possible, what each of these worldviews holds to be important and true about the world.

First, for theists: Their worldview is that humans were expressly created by God, and as such, are to act as co-regents with the Divine, to govern the Earth in truth and justice, as it's revealed in *The Bible*. However, due to the Fall of Man, the world and all its inhabitants have been plunged into a state of chaos, and so suffering, disease, and death have infected the human race. Since then, humanity and the world have only gradually been brought back into the original dominion of God, first through the death and resurrection of Christ and then through the agency of Christ's Church. Bottom line: Life has no meaning apart from the message contained in *The Bible*, therefore it behooves everyone to come to understand its message.

Next, for deists: Their worldview is that both humans and Nature, including all non-humans, were created by God with equal value, to co-exist on Earth in harmony, quite apart from any special revelation as espoused by theists. But because they typically reject the written word of God, they also reject the notion that divine judgment caused the chaos found in the world and instead interpret suffering, disease, and death as further proof of their belief in divine non-intervention. Bottom line: Life has no meaning apart from the message contained in the natural world, therefore it behooves everyone to come to understand its message.

And finally, for atheists: Their worldview is that, because there is no evidence of a divine creative entity, both humans and nature are products of brute, impersonal forces. As such, every living thing has inexplicably coalesced out of a primordial "chemical soup," as it were, to produce all the organisms on Earth. Based on this line of thinking, all suffering, disease, and death are neither the result of sin nor divine apathy but are instead the inevitable outcome of a world dominated as much by entropy and decay as natural selection and the survival of the fittest. The Universe is therefore devoid of any spiritual dimension or purpose, and so death is just as meaningless as life. Bottom line: Life has no meaning to be gathered from either *The Bible* or the natural world, therefore it behooves everyone to come to grips with that message.

With the foregoing worldviews in mind, we'll next examine in more detail the way each of them interprets suffering, disease, and death; however, as I alluded to earlier, we'll do this against the backdrop of that other all-important thing we've been examining, which is to say, the role that Nature plays in regard to each of these worldviews. And the reason we'll do this is because as I previously stated, without fully appreciating the role of Nature, all three of these worldviews are deficient in the very thing each group insists is important and true about the world.

In review, then: Theists see death as the "final enemy" from which God will one day deliver humanity and the

Universe, as all history moves toward the consummation of the ages as predicted in *The Bible*. Deists see death as a "tragic enemy" that touches every creature in the endless struggle for existence, but because the Great Clockmaker, in their view, has withdrawn His direct presence, the Universe has no hope of salvation as depicted in Scripture. And atheists see death as a "mindless enemy" that overtakes all lifeforms without judgment or providence, and because there is no rhyme or reason to what happens, in their view, death is neither to be feared nor hoped for.

As a result of these different worldviews, each group, as would be expected, reacts to death in their own way. However, as differently as these worldviews are from each other, they still hold one thing in common: they each in their own way seek an antidote to a common enemy. Strangely enough, though, if asked why they see death so differently, most would say it's because of their particular view concerning the question of God's existence or non-existence, and His involvement or non-involvement in the world. In short, theists seek a supernatural approach and so look to God's prophetic word that speaks of the resurrection of the dead; deists take a more natural approach to the physical world, where death is viewed as simply another aspect of the wheel of life; and atheists adopt a realistic approach and so ignore anything in Scripture or Nature as a form of comfort as that would set oneself up for certain disappointment.

However, as anyone who's been following along in our present investigation knows, more important than solving the mysteries of God's existence or non-existence and His involvement or non-involvement in the world, there is one's personal attitude about these mysteries, as in, whether one views them through the eyes of the hardcore cynic or the merely suspicious. Add to that the pivotal role that Nature plays in the matrix of life and death, and one must admit that all the old stereotypes simply fail to measure up the way they used to.

FIRST OF ALL, for those who consider themselves theists, remember what we talked about earlier, in that everything you hold near and dear in the way of biblical knowledge is still subject to interpretation whether you admit it or not. As such, your confidence in God's word will always be subject to your daily experiences, whether they be good, bad, or indifferent. That's why God's word is stricter in its judgment regarding the revelatory aspects of Nature as opposed to mankind's opinion of the written record of Scripture. This, of course, is something that many Christians will object to, stating their faith in Scripture is secure and so nothing can shake their confidence in it. But keep in mind, I'm not talking about one's faith in *The Bible* in the face of the typical challenges of the day. I'm talking about your faith being challenged when you've been kicked in the teeth because of the death of someone you love. Then naturally all bets are off. Theology is no longer in those moments something we assent to with just our heads; then it's something that strikes at the heart of our very being. It's then that our minds, which are typically in control, are suddenly sent reeling. It's then that we're in need of more than a fine sermon or a sympathetic word.

As for those who consider themselves deists, again, remember what we touched on earlier, in that despite the beauty and majesty of the natural world, according to your worldview, God never intervenes in the affairs of humanity. As such, your world is driven by heartless, mindless forces, where life and death are subject to brute force and violence, where the strong prey upon the weak, in an endless, vicious cycle. And to think that such a tragic worldview is the outcome of your reaction to seeing too many people being abusive, hypocritical, or tyrannical. And if God did care about humanity in the way that theists insist, then certainly He'd never allow such contradictions and cruelties to continue. Worse still, when the deist is rocked to his or her core, when personally touched by the death of a loved one, what kind of hope or comfort does their impersonal view of Nature provide them?

Then there are those who consider themselves atheists. Everything you hold near and dear is a world where there is no room for God because the natural world didn't require a Creator in the first place. Just because Nature seems to run like a clock doesn't mean you have to fall for such silliness as those who insist a clock implies a clockmaker. For you, the fact that there is no direct evidence of God's existence settles the matter succinctly. For you, the fact that the animal, plant, and mineral kingdoms seem to represent a great pyramidal structure where all life interconnects, from the lowest organisms right up to the highest primates is also sufficient reason for dismissing the need of a Creator. And for you, when death comes staring you in the face, you waste no time in the sentimental hogwash that gullible types insist on resorting to. Rather than drown yourself in pity and piety on behalf of the dead, you shield your heart like the good little soldier you see yourself to be.

Such is the power of your attitude to shape the world you live in, to shape the way you face your fate as a creature living in a world where death comes to all. However, as powerful as attitude is, whether in the form of trust or suspicion, hope or cynicism, there's still something to be said about scientific facts. In this case, I'm talking about facts that have been available, in varying degrees, to all three groups we've been examining. These facts involve something we've touched on throughout this investigation but will in this final leg of our journey look at in earnest, which is to say, the role that Nature plays in the world.

We've looked at it from the perspective of theists, deists, and atheists, in which Nature was originally the subject matter of natural philosophers beginning in seventeenth-century Europe. Then, as the processes of Nature became more and more available to humanity by way of the microscope, chemistry, and experimentation, Nature gradually shifted from being the domain of philosophers to that of scientists.

Parenthetically, we should note another of the great ironies of history, in which the work of Christian philosophers and naturalists like Boyle, Ray, Digby, Burnet, and Linnaeus, in pursuit of unlocking the mysteries of Nature, laid the foundations for modern science. Such connections, though, are rarely the subject of secular schools, where most wish to distort the true origins of science. The connection I'm speaking of will not only shock most people, but it will also prove vital to the conclusion of this work. Because in order to demonstrate the genuine role of Nature, in terms of God's revealed purposes, we'll have to return to what we were exploring earlier, which is to say, the economy of Nature.

Properly understood in all its dimensions, the concept of the economy of Nature speaks to humanity's deepest need in determining the truth about that dreaded enemy: death. In doing so, it also provides an antidote to that other enemy of humanity: cynicism. Without this antidote, the specter of death stands forth as the ultimate stain upon God's created world. Without this antidote, there is no adequate answer to the charge that this world is the imperfect product of a God Who, in allowing for this imperfection, appears to be the opposite of everything *The Bible* says about Him. If that's true, then cynics are correct when they insist that God isn't perfect, just as Mills once said of those who, in his view, offered their weak claims:

They have believed, perhaps, that God could, if He willed, remove all the thorns from their individual path, but not without causing greater harm to someone else, or frustrating some purpose of greater importance to the general well-being. They have believed that He could do any one thing, but not any combination of things: that His government, like human government, was a system of adjustments and compromises; that the world is inevitably imperfect, contrary to His intention.

The Idea of God in Nature

Quite apart from the accusations of deists, atheists have had a field day in their apparently correct view that a Supreme Being could never be responsible for the world we live in, therefore any claim of God being omnipotent is undermined by the presence of death in the Universe. Add to this the apparent absence of God in the world and no wonder an atheist like Charles Darwin was able to so easily sell his theory of evolution to the public.

The only problem, though, with Darwin's theory is something that no one espousing evolution ever wants to discuss. And that is, without the foundation of Ray's concept of species and Linnaeus' taxonomy of the biological world, Darwin would have had no foundation on which to build his work. First, Linnaeus wrote in his 1751 book:

> By the economy of Nature, we understand the all-wise disposition of the Creator in relation to natural things, by which they are fitted to produce general ends, and reciprocal uses...
>
> Whoever duly turns his attention to the things on our globe, must necessarily confess, that they are so connected, so chained together, that they all aim

at the same end, and to this end a vast number of intermediate ends are subservient.

The Economy of Nature

Then, more than a hundred years later, Darwin wrote in his 1859 book:

> All organic beings are striving, it may be said, to seize their own place in the economy of nature...
>
> And it follows, I think ... that the varying offspring of each species will try (only a few will succeed) to seize on as many and as diverse places in the economy of nature as possible. Each new variety or species, when formed, will generally take the place of and so exterminate its less well-fitted parent. This, I believe, to be the origin of the classification or arrangement of all organic beings at all times.
>
> *The Origin of Species*

Concerning the connection between the work of Linnaeus and Darwin in the latter's development of his evolutionary theory, Pence and Swaim cite:

> Given the twin roots of the economy of Nature in Linnaeus' theological convictions and Swedish economic policy, it is perhaps surprising that it is found throughout Darwin's work, Darwin being neither theologically inclined nor Swedish. But the concept appears early and often. Darwin read ... *The Economy of Nature* on the 13th of May, 1841. The early 1840s are an interesting moment in the development of Darwin's theory...
>
> Between the essentially complete formation of the theory and the first preparation of the *Sketch* in

1842, the *Sketch* contains the economy of Nature in essentially all the forms in which it would be found in Darwin's mature works. Darwin even describes the entire second part of the *Sketch*—corresponding to the last seven or so chapters of the *Origin*, in which Darwin considers both objections to and unexpected results which follow from common descent and natural selection—as "devoted to the general consideration of how far the economy of Nature justifies or opposes the belief that related species and genera are descended from common stocks."

> *The Economy of Nature: The Structure of Evolution in Linnaeus, Darwin, and Toward the Extended Synthesis*

Again, it would be a huge understatement to note the irony in how the role of Nature undergirds what I'm suggesting would benefit theists, deists, and atheists alike, of which this concept of the economy of Nature provides the linchpin. But before I fully expound what I've only been hinting at, I'd ask you to first consider something.

Consider how easy it would be to dismiss the idea that death could provide any beneficial effect if it were limited to just one group to the exclusion of the others. If that were the case, then one could simply chalk it up to wishful thinking on the part of anyone claiming such things. Or maybe it's just another example of self-deception, because naturally it's too good to be true and therefore one is right to be suspicious of such ideas. As such, the cynical mind would be perfectly justified for doubting such possibilities as being the stuff of myth or superstition. However, when we consider how the concept of the economy of Nature has moved, since the days of Digby and Linnaeus, beyond the realm of theology and has permeated even the modern scientific realm, we can't help but sit up and take notice.

AT ITS CORE, presently, the Economy of Nature speaks of the interconnectivity and interdependency of all life on this planet. Previously, the world had been seen primarily in mechanical terms, as separate systems comprised of an array of individual parts. As such, organisms were seen in purely biological terms, which isolated and partitioned its subject matter, whether in the way creatures themselves were viewed or the organs that comprised the creatures.

In contrast, the new view focuses on seeing the world in holistic terms, which is more and more being understood as an expansive whole that is greater than the sum of its parts. Now all forms of life, whether human or non-human, whether animal or plant, whether organic or inorganic, are being seen in ecological terms. No longer are organisms seen as independent of one another; they are all seen as being part of a "web of life," as it's been called by the Austrian-born American physicist Fritjof Capra. As Capra describes it:

> All members of an ecological community are interconnected in a vast and intricate network of relationships, the web of life. They derive their essential properties and, in fact, their very existence from their relationships to other things.
>
> *The Web of Life: A New Scientific Understanding of Living Systems*

Capra then goes on to describe how this new worldview isn't simply a matter of facts *per se*; it also entails our willingness or unwillingness, our ability or inability, to change our minds about the nature of reality. Capra goes on to say:

> Understanding ecological interdependence means understanding relationships. It requires the shifts of perception that are characteristic of systems think-

ing—from the parts to the whole, from objects to relationships, from contents to patterns.

The Web of Life: A New Scientific Understanding of Living Systems

In other words, it's not just what the facts of Nature present to our senses that matters, but it also involves our attitude toward the set of facts that we're confronted with. That's why I've repeatedly requested throughout this work that we examine our own attitudes in the process of my telling this story. Otherwise, acquired habits developed over a lifetime of experience might hinder our attempt at getting at the answers we're seeking.

As I've previously stated: It does no good to provide answers to the questions we're grappling with if our tendency toward cynicism prevents our appreciation of those answers. Naturally, I'd hope that my presentation of the so-called "facts" will be received objectively, but being all too aware of the power of cynicism, I'm doing all I can to anticipate its impact. That's why I'm trying to be as thorough as I can to lay out, piece by piece, what I hope to say.

Now at this point you might think that I'm splitting hairs, or perhaps that I'm stalling for time, in my not getting to the point faster. But remember what we're talking about here. This is some weighty subject matter that we're dealing with. An imperfect world created by a perfect God? Confronting the truth about mankind's most dreaded enemy: death? Hopefully you can appreciate my reluctance to simply blurt out my answer.

Just think of the implications of what I'm proposing: It's my belief that there's something common to the worldviews held by theists, deists, and atheists alike, which could make an incredible difference as to how all three groups see the world upon hearing about this "something." So far, we know that "something" involves how all three groups view the way death impacts our lives, but so far, all that I've presented are arguments based on either philosophy or theology.

I've pointed out how theists hope that death doesn't mean the end of existence but so far, we have only stories of various resurrections in *The Bible* like that of Lazarus and Jesus to confirm the possibility of such things. Then we have the deists who insist that Nature is the only tangible reality for the existence of God but even that falls short of expectation when those same people have no answer as to why a God Who can create the Universe can't communicate with His own creatures. And finally, we have the atheists who sit back and criticize anyone who they consider naïve enough to believe in any version of God, which they don't require because to them Nature is already quite sufficient enough.

As for the "something" that I believe offers hope to those who say they already have hope, and comfort to those who say they need no comfort, consider this: What if the amazing properties of Nature could provide a common point of interest—an "antidote," if you will—for all three groups? However, for these properties to be effective, all three groups would have to resist their natural tendency toward cynicism. Otherwise, if we allow the lens of cynicism to distort the facts as they exist, we can't help but fail to integrate these amazing properties into a broader view of the natural world.

With that in mind, let's return to our present take on how the economy of Nature has developed since the days of Linnaeus and Darwin, and entered the modern lexicon as the ecology of life. To make this point clearer, it should first be remembered how Darwin built his theoretical model directly upon the work of Ray and Linnaeus. We see this in the choice of words that Darwin used, in echoing such concepts as the role of "species" in the physical descent of plants and animals, as well as the "economy of nature" in the organization of the descent of the various species of plants and animals. In this way, we can clearly recognize that the modern pursuit of ecology is simply a continuation of this concept of the economy of Nature, but one that was literally dissected from its theological roots.

We see the same thing when in 1866 Ernst Haeckel, called the "German Darwin," chose the word "ecology" for the "new science" of studying the Earth and all its organisms. As Haeckel himself described it:

> By ecology we mean the body of knowledge concerning the economy of nature—the investigation of the total relations of the animal both to the inorganic and to its organic environment; including, above all, its friendly and inimical relations with those animals and plants with which it comes directly or indirectly into contact—in a word, ecology is the study of all those complex interrelations referred to by Darwin as the conditions of the struggle for existence.
>
> *Principles of Animal Ecology*

This idea is further illustrated when we note that both words, "economy" and "ecology," are derived from the same Greek word *oikos*, which means "home." In the case of economy, there is added the word *nomos*, which means "management" or "regulation." As such, economy speaks of "home management," and so in this context, describes how the natural world, though unruly and hostile on many levels, still reveals a managerial aspect to it in the way that animals, plants, and minerals display an underlying interconnectedness. As for ecology, there is the added word *logia*, which means "knowledge" or "study." And so, ecology speaks of the study of the Earth as being the home of all forms of life. It's also interesting that both *nomos* and *logia* denote that their subject matter is not to be seen as being of a random nature but, rather, something that exhibits clear patterns that can be mapped out and codified.

Next, in this progressive movement from economy to ecology, we see over the course of time how the natural world went from being viewed philosophically and theologically to one that is now viewed scientifically and empirically. Whereas in previous centuries the economy of Nature described the interconnectedness of all lifeforms on a strictly surface level, nowadays the web of life can be observed, with the aid of technology, on a minutely microbial level. In short, what eighteenth-century thinkers like Linnaeus perceived intuitively, twenty-first-century thinkers like Capra perceive inductively.

In this case, in our search for an antidote common to all three of the groups we're examining, we'll return to our investigation of how death and birth play out a timeless pattern in the natural world. To most observers throughout history, the events surrounding the death and birth of Earth's lifeforms has typically appeared to be entirely random; however, to those who pay close attention, they reveal highly specific patterns of a cyclical nature. We repeatedly see this in the ecology of the Earth's biosphere, where even in death matter is never lost; it's always recycled from one level of life to another. In short, without the death of one organism, a myriad of other lifeforms could never be born, grow, or live. Biologists and ecologists call it the nutrient cycle, or as Elizabeth McDuffie describes it, "the process through which death is used to sustain life." According to Cain, Bowman, and Hacker:

> The cyclic movement of nutrients such as nitrogen or phosphorus between organisms and the physical environment is referred to as the nutrient cycle. Life would cease if nutrients were not recycled because

the molecules that organisms need for their growth and reproduction would not be available to them...

All organisms in an ecosystem are either consumed by other organisms at higher trophic levels or enter the pool of dead organic matter, or detritus. In most terrestrial ecosystems, only a relatively small proportion of the biomass is consumed, and most of the energy flow passes through detritus (i.e., dead plants, animals, and microorganisms). Because most of this energy flow occurs in the soil, we are not always aware of its magnitude and importance.

> *Ecology*

As such, what is now labeled a "nutrient cycle" reveals far more than meets the eye. As McDuffie describes it:

Life exists as systems, and systems within systems... Within each system, there are cycles that allow for the continuation of the system. The nutrient cycle is a vital cycle within each system...

Therefore, death is a vital aspect of the nutrient cycle, and thus, a vital aspect of the resurrection of new life on Earth. Organisms live together in communities. Within the community, nutrient cycles occur and allow for the passing of material nutrients and support of new life for the continuation of the community. The necessity of nutrient cycles demonstrates that living communities are dependent on the death and decay involved in such cycles to create and sustain ecosystems.

> *Ecology and Theology in Dialogue: Death and Resurrection from an Ecological and Theological Perspective*

Notice here how McDuffie doesn't just speak of this nutrient cycle as a brute, impersonal aspect of living systems. Instead, she describes it in terms of "the resurrection of life" and "the continuation of the community." For McDuffie, then, the processes of the natural world reveal more than mere ecological forces; they have theological implications as well, as she goes on to say:

> Both ecology and theology speak to death and resurrection of life. Biblically informed theology tells us that resurrection is of a different substance than life— our very "selves" will be wholly resurrected and will be made everlasting—an entirely new structure of created order and thus, a new ecology will ensue upon resurrection. In ecology, resurrection takes the form of carbon cycles, matter is transformed and resurrected in and of this world rather than the next, which involves a constant renewal of the Earth we currently inhabit.
>
> Contrary to cultural beliefs and fears, ecology helps people to see death as a necessary and good process of ecological renewal on two levels because in ecology, death is the only means to both renewal and perpetuation of life.
>
> *Ecology and Theology in Dialogue: Death and Resurrection from an Ecological and Theological Perspective*

This, however, stands in sharp contrast to Capra, who also speaks of the pivotal role that nutrient cycles play in Earth's ecological systems but, in looking at the very same processes of Nature, he comes to a different conclusion:

> The cyclical nature of ecological processes is an important principle of ecology. The ecosystem's feed-

back loops are the pathways along which nutrients are continually recycled. Being open systems, all organisms in an ecosystem produce wastes, but what is waste for one species is food for another, so that the ecosystem as a whole remains without waste. Communities of organisms have evolved in this way over billions of years, continually using and recycling the same molecules of minerals, water, and air.

The Web of Life: A New Scientific Understanding of Living Systems

So whereas McDuffie speaks of this nutrient cycle in theological terms, Capra speaks of it in evolutionary terms. Such is the power of attitude, as we've repeatedly seen; such is the power of one's worldview in interpreting differently the very same set of "facts." Both McDuffie and Capra use the same words to describe these processes: nutrients, cycles, communities, ecology. But while Capra reduces it all to being the mindless product of evolutionary forces, McDuffie sees it all as being the mindful product of divine forces.

Notwithstanding such divergent interpretations of the same set of facts, there is still much to be said about their similarities, and it is because these worldviews are so similar, despite their obvious differences, that I'd like to suggest a more integrated approach to our view of the evidence so that all three groups—theists, deists, and atheists—can enrich their mutual search for meaning and truth.

CHAPTER ELEVEN

The Death of Beauty

(Because Real Hope isn't Something You Keep in Your Pocket Like a Lucky Rabbit's Foot)

> **OPTIMISM,** *a noun*
> "The doctrine, or belief, that everything is beautiful, including what is ugly, everything good, especially the bad, and everything right that is wrong... Being a blind faith, it is inaccessible to the light of disproof—an intellectual disorder, yielding to no treatment but death. It is hereditary, but fortunately not contagious."
>
> *The Cynic's Word Book,* Ambrose Bierce

IN CONFRONTING the carnivorous aspect of Nature, I can't help agreeing with Mill—in principle, at least—that it's not a pleasant thing to look upon. In fact it's downright abhorrent when you see the weak relentlessly preyed upon by the strong. Loving animals as much as I do, I regularly cry out to God to end the vicious cycle of the killing of innocent creatures. Just because Adam rebelled against God, why, I wonder, do others have to suffer the consequences that have befallen them through no fault of their own.

In this case, I'm one of those self-characterized theists who have an incredibly difficult time stomaching the presence of any kind of death—human or otherwise—in an otherwise beautiful creation. As a Christian who is familiar with *The Bible*, I'm well aware of passages that speak of the present predicament of the world and the hope that one day things will be set right. Said the Apostle Paul:

> I consider that our present sufferings can't compare with the glory that will be revealed in us. For the creation waits in eager expectation for the children of God to be revealed. For the creation was subjected to frustration, not by its own choice, but by the will of the one who subjected it, in hope that the creation itself will be liberated from its bondage to decay and brought into the freedom and glory of the children of God.
>
> We know that the whole creation has been groaning as in the pains of childbirth right up to the present time. Not only does it groan, but we ourselves groan inwardly as we, who have the first fruits of the Spirit, wait eagerly for our adoption into His family through the redemption of our bodies. For in this hope, we were saved. But hope that is seen isn't hope at all. Who hopes for what they already have? But if we hope for what we don't have yet, we wait for it patiently.
>
> *The Book of Romans*

But until that day arrives, there isn't much else we can do except place our hope in that promise ... and wait. Until then, the world is such that man is against animal, animal is against animal, animal is against man, man is against nature, nature is against man, and man is against man. As Bierce, our resident cynic, described it, although in his decidedly egocentric way:

In all the world there is no city of refuge—no temple in which to take sanctuary, clinging to the horns of the altar—no "place apart" where, like hunted deer, we can hope to elude the baying pack of Nature's malevolences. The dead-line is drawn at the gate of life: Man crosses it at birth. His advent is a challenge to the entire pack—earthquake, storm, fire, flood, drought, heat, cold, wild beasts, venomous reptiles, noxious insects, bacilli, spectacular plague and velvet-footed household disease—all are fierce and tireless in pursuit. Dodge, turn, and double how he can, there's no eluding them; sooner or later some of them have him by the throat and his spirit returns to the God who gave it ... and gave them.

A Cynic Looks at Life

For a hardcore cynic like Bierce, then, the world as it exists could never be anything but an imperfect place where even when he does refer to God, he does so mockingly. As for the world being something good given to us by a God of goodness, he continued:

We are told that this Earth was made for our inhabiting. Our dearly beloved brethren in the faith, our spiritual guides, philosophers, and friends of the pulpit, never tire of pointing out the goodness of God in giving us so excellent a place to live in and commending the admirable adaptation of all things to our needs.

What a fine world it is, to be sure—a darling little world, "so suited to the needs of man." A globe of liquid fire, straining within a shell relatively no thicker than that of an egg—a shell constantly cracking and in momentary danger of going all to pieces! Three-fourths of this electable field of human activity are covered with an element in which we can't breathe, and which swallows us by myriads: With moldering bones the deep is white; from the frozen zones to the tropic bright.

A Cynic Looks at Life

And in mocking the notion of the Earth being created out of God's goodness, or of the Earth's ecosystem revealing a remarkable penchant for rebirth and renewal, we'd naturally understand this kind of thinking from an unabashed atheist and cynic like Bierce.

Again and again, we've seen how our worldview inevitably shapes the world we live in, and in this we're reminded of the old adage: "Beauty is in the eye of the beholder." As such, while others may genuinely appreciate what is beautiful, the cynical mind sees something else. According to Bierce: "Beauty" is defined as "the power by which a woman charms a lover and terrifies a husband." And: "Bait" is defined as "a preparation that renders the hook more palatable. The best kind is beauty." As to why Bierce would say this about beauty, we may have a clue in something else he said: "The creator and arbiter of beauty is the heart; to the male rattlesnake the female rattlesnake is the loveliest thing in nature."

Of course, the irony of Bierce's penetrating observations is that he's not entirely wrong in being suspicious of the human heart, considering its pernicious tendency toward foolishness, hypocrisy, and pride. Naturally, this was something that Jesus and the prophets constantly warned us about. However, where the merely suspicious are forewarned and resist the darker aspects of our human nature, the hardcore cynic is incapable of determining when it's actually safe to embrace such things as truth, beauty, and justice. As such, wherever the cynical eye looks, it sees only the veil of negativity that so often obscures the true nature of the positivity behind it. Wherever the cynical eye looks, it sees only the pain and suffering of the fallen creation around us. Wherever it looks, then, it's incapable of seeing the inherent beauty of God's natural world; it sees only the death of beauty.

That said, it would be instructive to examine just how the eye of cynicism shaped the worldview of three of our most prominent players: Linnaeus, the theist; Paine, the deist; and Bierce, the atheist.

IN HINDSIGHT, it's easy to see how numerous events in Ambrose Bierce's life predisposed him to cynicism. His life is a classic example of hope disappointed, born as he was into a family whose ancestors came to America in 1620 on the *Mayflower* as part of the Great Puritan Migration. On one hand, Bierce followed in his father's footsteps, a printer in an abolitionist newspaper, as can be seen in his initial eagerness to enlist in the Union Army in the Civil War. On the other hand, he chafed at his Puritan upbringing and was especially critical of his illustrious heritage that included his mother being a descendant of none other than the seventeenth-century English Puritan Separatist William Bradford.

Add to that, Bierce faced a great deal of tragedy in his personal life, with his two sons dying prematurely and his marriage ending in failure. His oldest son died by his own hand after being rejected romantically, and his other son died from pneumonia complicated by alcoholism. His ex-wife died the following year. He also endured lifelong physical disabilities like asthma, as well as fainting spells as a result of a head wound that he sustained while fighting for the Union cause at Kennesaw Mountain.

But apart from all his personal issues, both physical and familial, what most impacted Bierce was the psychological impact of war itself, as Bierce's biographer, Richard O'Connor, sees it:

> War was the making of Bierce as a man and a writer... He became truly capable of transferring the bloody, headless bodies and boar-eaten corpses of the battlefield onto paper.
>
> *The Good, the Bad and the Mad*

As a result of all this, Bierce went from being the idealistic child of abolition to the cynical critic of anyone naïve enough to believe in such tripe as patriotism, which he defined as: "Combustible rubbish ready to torch anyone ambitious enough to illuminate his name." One can only wonder, though, when saying such things, was he really talking about others, whom he outwardly mocked? Or was he instead looking into the mirror of his own soul and speaking of himself, inwardly, when he described a patriot as: "The dupe of statesmen and the tool of conquerors."

But what about deists and theists like Paine and Linnaeus? Certainly they would never think to disparage God. But as it so happened, they too, at times, leaned each in their own way toward what can only be described as a darkened worldview. And mind you, this dark view was derived from the fact that all three men had something in common: Each one of them was traumatized by the death of loved ones.

In both his private and public life, Thomas Paine was a man of contradictions; as such, he was a perfect vessel for the cynical mind. His formative years were marked by two important features: his sister died while still in her infancy, when Thomas was not much more than two, and he was the child of quarreling parents who each viewed Christianity in different ways. So, while his sister's untimely passing meant the death of his only sibling, his parents' argumentativeness meant the death of a stable and happy childhood.

The root cause of his parents' arguing came down to one thing: Paine's father was a Quaker, and his mother was an Anglican. In many ways, then, Paine's personal contradictions perfectly mirrored the conflict between his parents' divergent views of Christianity. Anglicans view humans as being inherently corrupt, naturally inclined toward evil, and incapable of choosing God for themselves. Quakers, on the other hand, believe humans are inherently good, and that God resides in everyone. Anglicans believe churches should be dependent and governed by its bishops, while Quakers believe churches should be independent and governed by its members. Anglicans confess their sins to a priest, while Quakers confess their sins directly to God. Seen against this backdrop, it's clear that Paine's worldview as an adult reveals an allegiance to his father's way of thinking, and a rebellion against his mother's worldview.

Prior to his success in Revolutionary America, Paine was by some accounts either a failure or cursed in his country of origin: England. For more than twenty years, he failed or was unhappy in every job he attempted. In 1759, Paine happily married but shortly thereafter his business failed. Soon, his wife Mary became pregnant, but when she went into early labor, both she and their baby daughter died. Then in 1774, his next marriage failed just as he set sail for colonial America, and so ended a grim chapter in his life, where he'd lost every job, business, sibling, wife, or child he had ever had.

Although he eventually succeeded on behalf of America's revolutionary cause, with such important works as *Common Sense*, his contradictory ways continued, particularly whenever the subject involved religious matters. While he insisted: "I believe in one God, and no more; and I hope for happiness beyond this life," yet in stating his case for deism and the divinity of Nature, he denied the divine authorship of *The Bible*. But not content to simply dismiss its contents as irrelevant, Paine stated that "it would be more consistent if we call it the word of a demon than the word of God." Then, no sooner had he said that then he referenced it as though it were a valid source, predicting that his generation "would appear to the future as the Adam of a new world." In his most famous work of all, he built his case concerning the so-called "right of kings" firmly on the foundation of *The Bible*, where he stated:

> As the exalting of one man so greatly above the rest cannot be justified on the equal rights of Nature, so neither can it be defended on the authority of Scripture.
>
> *Common Sense*

On still another occasion, he made similar reference, using biblical terminology, in which he stated:

> Tyranny, like Hell, is not easily conquered; yet we have this consolation with us, that the harder the conflict, the more glorious the triumph…
>
> Heaven knows how to put a proper price upon its goods; and it would be strange indeed if so celestial an article as freedom should not be highly rated.
>
> *The American Crisis*

Imagine that. A man well known for his antagonism toward *The Bible*, yet when it came right down to it, Paine didn't hesitate to turn to it when it aided his cause. Heaven, Hell, celestial articles, the authority of Scripture—all ideas lifted from a text that Paine elsewhere claimed should be called "the work of a demon rather than the word of God." Sounds like another man who was just as inconsistent when it came to his thoughts on God and Nature. While it's said of Mill that no one was more eloquent about the ethical virtues of Jesus of Nazareth, when it came to his view of Nature, it could only be "the work of a demon and not that of a Being of infinite power."

So, while men like Digby and Linnaeus saw the creation in terms of its economic harmony, Paine and Mill saw Nature and Scripture as being the work of a demon. But in response to such hyperbole, we have to ask: How would Paine and Mill have responded to the question of what could a demon know about things like rebirth and renewal as they're depicted in both Nature and Scripture? Then, quite apart from how a demon could know of such things, what does a demon know about creating such a world, where death provides the building blocks of rebirth, or as McDuffie describes it, of the resurrection of life? Clearly, what we have here, then, is another instance of how cynicism dramatically alters one's worldview even when that person is normally level-headed about every other arena of life.

Finally, we'll look at how the death of a loved one negatively impacted even a theist like Carl Linnaeus. More than anyone else, Linnaeus was someone who was responsible for seeing death in the natural world in a way that we might suggest is how God Himself sees it—a man who succinctly described death not as an end of life but as a segue to new life. That, together with the promises in *The Bible*, and certainly this was someone who would never be discouraged when visited by death, not even the death of a loved one. However, nothing could be further from the truth.

For Linnaeus, death was no stranger. In 1744, his daughter Sara Lena died after only living fifteen days. Thirteen years later, his son Johannis died of whooping cough, not yet three years old, at the age when "he had just begun to say a few words." According to biographer Lisbet Koerner, Linnaeus came to fear the birth of any more children into his family. He wrote in 1758:

I am a child of misfortune; if I had a rope and English courage, I would have hung myself long ago. I fear my wife is pregnant again.

Linnaeus: Nature and Nation

Death touching him so intimately, Linnaeus developed a peculiar split in regard to humanity's place in the divine economy of Nature. On one hand, Linnaeus believed that humans were "the final goal of creation … the Almighty's masterpiece, placed on this globe." On the other hand, he lamented:

Nothing is frailer than human life, nothing so vulnerable to so many diseases, so many troubles, so many dangers…

Old age is filled with pain, then the senses darken, the limbs grow numb; sight, hearing, movement, and the teeth—the tools for eating—die before you do.

The System of Nature

As a result of such cynicism, Linnaeus came to wonder why God created us "more miserable than any other animal," even while we live in the midst of a Nature that otherwise reveals such a divine economy. In short, rather than seeing suffering, disease, and death through the prism of what he knew about the natural world, Linnaeus sadly never seems to have benefited from his own philosophy when it came to confronting such things in his own life.

FOR ALL three men, then, life seen through the lens of cynicism offered little hope of expecting anything better. That's because, like most intangibles in life—such as faith and love—real hope isn't something you keep in your pocket like a lucky rabbit's foot. Real hope is something far more elusive, because hope is never static; it waxes and wanes over time. Correctly understood, hope is like a ship on the ocean, with waves sometimes calm, sometimes fierce. As such, some days our hope is clear and tangible, but on other days, foggy and vague. That's why it's so important to have something to augment our view of *The Bible*—in the process of waiting on God's promises—which is why I'm always looking to anchor my hope in anything God might have provided along the way in our journey of faith.

However, just as there is both blind faith and real faith, there's also false hope and real hope. That's why I'm so keen on zeroing in on more than nice sounding platitudes of believing in such intangibles as the hope of resurrection. That's why I'm convinced that if there's any truth to our being adopted into God's family, and our receiving a body of resurrection, then there must be tangible clues to that future by virtue of this world having been created by the same God Who made such promises of this future life.

In short, then, what evidence in this life is there concerning that future one? More importantly, what evidence is there that speaks to the concerns not only of theists but also of deists and atheists. After all, if there's any truth to the fact that God wishes that no one should perish, then wouldn't He provide universal evidence of that calling to more than those who are already convinced of His revelation? This is, of course, why I've been persistently presenting the physical evidence for a pattern of death and resurrection in the ecological processes of the Earth. If this evidence is valid, then there's much more to God's promise concerning the resurrection of the dead than what is contained in the written testimony of Scripture.

In examining this universal evidence, though, I think we need to address one more thing before closing out our investigation. We need to ask ourselves: In analyzing this evidence, what do we expect to find? Do we assume that we'll find the answer to what is most important to us? Or if we understand that the creation was created by a Creator, do we, instead, assume we'll find an answer that is most important to the Creator? Oddly enough this seems to be a much-overlooked approach to our quest for the meaning of life. That's because whenever we ask questions like these, it's typically assumed that if we answer them, our answers will revolve around us and our need to become what we're destined to become.

But rarely, if ever, do we think of this quest for meaning in terms of what the Creator considers important. Naturally when we ask about such things, they can be boiled down to a single line of questioning, which is: In our quest to determine if our imperfect world is still the product of a perfect God, how are we to understand the true meaning of human destiny? Ultimately, the question always comes down to this, because whenever we talk about human destiny, we instinctively realize there's no point in even talking about it if we're unable to resolve the paradox of God's perfect will even in the midst of this imperfect world. Therefore, our quest isn't just to discover what our destiny is as we envision it; we need to discover what our destiny is as it has been determined by the One Who created us. Which in turn brings me to the ultimate twist in this whole line of questioning.

Being human such as we are, and tending always to judge matters in terms of how they impact us for good or bad, I'd like to take a moment to flip the script on this question concerning our so-called "imperfect world" and whether or not that imperfection should reflect on God's perfection. Try asking this: What if, because we're human, our interpretation of this whole question is upside down? And what if, by presuming to judge God based on the imperfection of this world, our view of things turns out to be wrong? What do I mean by that? Well, try for once looking at the whole affair, not based on your desires and dreams but, rather, try looking at it from God's perspective.

So, in asking whether a perfect God has failed because we live in an imperfect world, let's begin by analyzing such concepts as are expressed in this discussion. First, let's define the word "perfect." When we discuss the idea of something being "perfect," who's idea of "perfection" are we talking about? Is it a perfect world only when that world is free from suffering, disease, or death, without sadness, darkness, or pain? Certainly that's what we've always assumed. But what if in assuming such things, we're actually sabotaging the very thing we're trying to accomplish?

What if instead of seeing the world as being "imperfect," why not try to see things differently? By that I mean, try to see things not as humans see them but, instead, try to see things the way that God might see them. In that case, wouldn't it be more accurate to say that a perfect world is one in which we're partaking of the same mode of existence as God? And so, maybe, along that line of reasoning, we need to see things as a parent sees them. We need to see that it's more important for our children to live a life in all its fullness, in all its dualities, as opposed to a stagnant and safe normality. But to do that, we'd have to allow our children to fail as much as they succeeded, to cry as much as they laughed, to suffer as much as they rejoiced, to die as much as they lived.

As such, the place where these conditions exist isn't some unknown world of the distant future; it's the world as God has designed it to exist in the here and now. In other words, the world we presently live in is such that even with all its flaws it's one in which God is somehow working out an end result that was never possible had we not first lost our innocence in the Garden. In short, it's a world that could never be perfect in an instant, but instead required the entrance of evil into the world as a result of free-willed beings that succumb so easily to it.

But having allowed suffering, disease, and death to enter the world, God also knew exactly how to transcend this situation, and so the world as we now experience it is proof of that very fact—a world where suffering, disease, and death don't simply produce what these free-willed beings expect from their limited perspective. Instead, they produce, as a result of God entering into every dimension of life and death, something altogether different. Rather than evil pronouncing our final doom, evil ironically serves as the ultimate tool in purging the sin of rebellion which lies at the heart of all the world's miseries and woes.

As for the greatest example of this reversal of fortune, the writer to the Hebrews explained:

> But we see Jesus, Who was made a little lower than the angels, now crowned with glory and honor because He suffered death, so that by the grace of God He might taste death for everyone.
>
> In bringing many children to glory, it was fitting for God, for Whom and through Whom all things exist, to make the author of their salvation perfect through suffering.
>
> *The Book of Hebrews*

In this, we see another marvelous example of how, from God's perspective, suffering, disease, and death aren't the same as we think of them. From God's perspective, they are vehicles by which the members of His family in Christ are "made perfect." In this case, the word used here doesn't speak of moral perfection as much as it does of "completion." From the Greek root word *telos*, this "completing" describes the process by which someone is being raised to a state that befits him or her.

Naturally, in the case of Jesus, the notion that He was "made perfect" only in the act of sacrificing Himself is contradictory to the context of Scripture as a whole. The only logical meaning, then, is that the perfection spoken of here is one in terms of His passion and death fulfilling His purpose and mission as a sacrifice for the sins of humanity. We understand this in what Christ spoke on the cross at the moment of His passing from this life: "It is finished."

As for the human members of God's family, this being "made perfect" describes a different kind of "completion," no doubt a lesser kind of perfection yet no less complete. Said the Apostle Peter:

> But the God of all grace, Who has called us to His eternal glory by Christ Jesus, after you have suffered a while, make you perfect, established, strengthened, and settled.
>
> *The First Book of Peter*

In this verse, Peter wasn't saying what most assume when they think of someone being "made perfect." Again, when most of us think of "perfection," we think of a world without suffering or sadness, without fear or pain. But here the Greek word that Peter used is *katartios*, which speaks of "being made ready," or "being equipped or furnished with the necessary tools." What's more, according to *The Strong's Exhaustive Concordance of The Bible*, this word used in our English Bibles for "perfect" also speaks of "being brought into its proper condition, whether for the first time, or after a lapse," "to mend what has been broken or rent," or "to make one what he ought to be, of one who by correction may be brought back into the right, or harmonious, way."

Clearly, then, when the question is asked concerning the true nature of this world and our destiny, especially as it relates to the presence of suffering, disease, and death, we might now see things differently. As opposed to trying to avoid everything humans dread, we might instead see them from God's perspective, in that what we fear the most actually produces in us the very thing we need the most. Then maybe we'll begin to see our present world, with so much pain and suffering, in a much different light. In this I'm reminded of another old adage that states: "It's not the bad thing itself that makes you or breaks you. It's whether it drives you toward God, or away from Him. If it drives you away from Him, it'll break you; but if it drives you toward Him, it'll make you."

Now mind you, I'm not saying that this world of suffering, disease, and death will exist in its present state forever; that, naturally, is something that God has also made provision for in due time. But in settling the question as adequately as is humanly possible, we can at least carry on with our lives so that with a clearer understanding of what it means to live life, and to live it more abundantly, we can avoid the sweet temptation of cynicism. When easy cynicism raises its ugly head in an attempt to turn the beauty of life and of the Earth into something it's not, we can remind it of what Job reminded his cynical friends when they tried to get him to see things their way:

> Ask the animals, and they'll instruct you; ask the birds of the air, and they'll tell you. Or speak to the Earth, and it will teach you; let the fish of the sea inform you. Which of all these doesn't know that the hand of the Lord has done this?
>
> *The Book of Job*

Ever since humans have pondered this biblical passage, there has been a difference of opinion as to its true meaning. On one side of the argument, certain commentators echo the sentiments of natural theologians like Ray and Linnaeus, who point to the design aspect of Nature in this way:

If appeal were made to the animal creation, and they were asked their position with respect to God, they would with one voice proclaim Him their absolute Ruler and Director. Ask the fowls of the air, and they will tell you. The instincts of birds, their periodical migrations, their inherited habits, are as wonderful as anything in the divine economy of the Universe, and as much imply God's continually directing hand.

The Pulpit Commentary

Or as another biblical commentator put it:

The beasts of the Earth, the fowls of the air, the fishes of the sea, all animals, and even plants, fruits, and flowers, are daily and hourly evidences to us, of the being and infinite perfections of God. The wonderful contrivance and admirable mechanism manifested in their formation, the preparation made for their wants, the exact adaptation of their organs to the particular mode of life for which they are intended; the wonderful regularity observed in their propagation: these things plainly tell us, they are the work of God, as if they all had intelligible voices and declared it to us.

The Benson Commentary

On the other hand, there is that other side of the argument, which aligns more accurately with the context of the conversation in *Job*, considering Job's comment regarding how "the tents of robbers are safe, and those who provoke God are secure—those whose god is in their fists." As the commentators continue in their thinking:

Some suppose that Job referred here to the greater and stronger brute creatures, preying on the lesser and weaker, as a fact illustrative of his argument respecting the power and prosperity of robbers, oppressors, and tyrants; and to the inferior animals in general, ministering to the pride, luxury, and indulgence of ungodly men; the Earth and its richest produce being their property, and all Nature drudging, as it were, to gratify their lusts. But the following verses seem rather to lead to the interpretation first mentioned, which certainly is the more instructive use of the words.

The Benson Commentary

Instructive or not, I'd suggest that based, as I've said, on the context of the biblical passage in question, I'd have to point to the latter interpretation. Recall the flow of the whole conversation, if you will, in which Job's friends mocked Job for insisting that he must be guilty because of the way he was suffering. Or else God would be unjust, in their view. But in response to their crass assumptions, which I'm insisting are more a function of the joy of cynicism than anything else, Job essentially told them, "Well, if you don't believe I'm innocent, just look at the animals all around you. Which of them are guilty of a crime? Yet their innocence doesn't rescue them from suffering, disease, or death." Or to point to yet another commentator who holds to the latter interpretation:

> Lions, wolves, and panthers are prospered—the lamb, the kid, the gazelle, are the victims... The object of Job is to show that rewards and punishments are not distributed according to character. This was so plain in his view as scarcely to argue the point. It was seen all over the world not only among people, but even in the brute creation. Everywhere the strong prey upon the weak; the fierce

upon the tame; the violent upon the timid. Yet God does not come forth to destroy the lion and the hyena, or to deliver the lamb and the gazelle from their grasp. Like robbers—lions, panthers, wolves, prowl upon the Earth; the eagle and the vulture from the air pounce upon the defenseless, and the great robbers of the deep prey upon the feeble, and still they prosper. What a striking illustration of the course of events among people, and of the relative condition of the righteous and the wicked.

Barnes' Notes on The Bible

All this reminds me of my own sense of outrage when it comes to my human desire for perfection and justice. Just as cynics like Bierce decry this world's dire predicament, in which he speaks of the "baying pack of Nature's malevolences," with its "wild beasts, venomous reptiles, and noxious insects," I'd like to add my own list of outrages. But while Bierce seems to be concerned only for adult human victims who he clearly holds in contempt for their general foolishness, my list of outrages includes everyone and everything else that I understand to be innocent even in the aftermath of Adam's fall. That's because while much of the pain and suffering most of us experience is nothing more than what we bring on ourselves, what I grieve most for are those who are clearly innocent of any wrongdoing.

In this I'm speaking just as much for all the animals who are subject to the principle of "dog-eat-dog," as I am for all humans who are among the less fortunate. Of course I'm talking about any number of tragedies like victims of abuse from without and from within, whether that involves defects of mind or body that occur either before or after birth. In this frustration, I'm in such agreement with Mill that it disturbs me, but there it is. Only when I confront the plight of those innocent ones do I find myself railing against

God and His apparent non-involvement in the world. Daily I cry out: But what about the children, Lord? Victims of child abuse or human trafficking? Or when animals are abused by those who exploit them for gain or sadistic pleasure? How can You idly sit by and allow such atrocities? How much longer must we endure these horrors?

Of course, while I may align myself with Mill's frustration over the agony of the creation, I choose not to subscribe to outright cynicism. Naturally, this is because of what I believe to be true about God's control over the Universe and His ability to transcend all that is negative as a result of Adam's fall. Naturally that's been the point of this entire work, to demonstrate that while sin and death may have been allowed to enter the world, God is still capable of offsetting that evil.

So, for me, the only answer to human and animal suffering is God's ability to transcend death and turn it into the resurrection of new life. This, in my view, leads me to one conclusion, echoing Paul's thoughts: I choose to focus on how the temporary pain and suffering that free will causes us precedes the ultimate act of God's grace and faithfulness whereby He makes restitution for all in all through the power of resurrection. And until that happens for every living thing, and whenever doubt and disappointment clouds that hope of resurrection, all I need to do is remember how the natural world daily displays this all-encompassing reality. And so, to echo Job once more:

> Which of all these doesn't know that the hand of the Lord has done this? The life of every living thing is in His hand, as well as the breath of all mankind.
>
> *The Book of Job*

And just in case anyone insists that *The Bible* only holds out the promise of resurrection to believers in Christ, please take note of what this verse is saying in the Hebrew language. When Job speaks of the "life" of every living thing, the word is *nephesh*, which according to *Strong's Concordance* speaks of "a soul, a living being, a life, a self, a person." In contrast, when Job speaks of the "breath" of all mankind, the word is *ruach*, which speaks of "breath, wind, spirit." Consider the irony of this choice of words in Scripture. Wouldn't we expect to see the opposite, based on the typical view that humans are made in the image of God and so exclusively have souls, but that animals—and all living things, for that matter—are nothing more than automatons and so are without souls? Either the traditional biblical worldview is correct, or *The Bible* itself is correct; which do you believe is correct?

Personally, I see this idea of every living thing as possessing the divine spark normally equated with humans alone as perfectly corresponding to the new view of the world as being a "web of life," in which every organism—human and non-human—is miraculously intertwined and interdependent with one another. Otherwise, why else would God—by way of the drama of Christ's death and resurrection—parallel this phenomenon in the very processes of Earth's biosphere, of death and rebirth, of death and resurrection? And not for the sake of humans alone, but for the sake of all living creatures?

Finally, in describing the world in this context, where humans may be incorrect about what is "perfect," and inaccurate about what is "just," we might hopefully formulate a new way of seeing things and so take a new approach in reassuring anyone struggling to cope with this stark world of ours with all its cruelties.

To any atheists like Bierce, we can point to a brand-new way of viewing their world that until now was only seen as being ruled by brute forces, and where death spelled the end of life in a vicious cycle of the survival of the fittest. Yet within the matrix of life and death, a marvelous confluence of every organism is displayed in which death is merely the prelude to rebirth and renewal. To them I'd ask: Is this what we'd expect from a godless Universe? How improbable is it really that this principle of the economy of Nature could simply evolve out of chaos with no hand to guide it?

To any deists like Paine, we can offer a new way of seeing their world, in which the weak are supplanted by the strong, and in which a Universe, apparently abandoned by God, nevertheless reveals a higher truth than ever deemed possible. To them I'd ask: Is this what we'd expect from a Universe created by a disinterested Creator? How improbable is it that if God can manifest this drama of death and resurrection in the creation itself that He can't also interject the same kinds of miracles described in *The Bible*?

And to any theists like Linnaeus, we can share another view of their world that sheds new light on an old truth, in which the hope of a future life is strengthened because of how God is demonstrating in this life the extent to which death is the ultimate doorway that leads to the resurrection of life. To them I'd ask: Is this what we'd expect in a Universe where God wasn't touched by our daily struggle of faith? How improbable is it that this process of death and rebirth would exist in the natural world if not to confirm our hope in the ultimate consummation of the ages?

How different, then, are these ideas of perfection and of a perfect world from what most believe when thinking of the present state of our world. How different are they from what we traditionally think of in terms of what it means to be resurrected and who is worthy of being resurrected. Yet I can think of no better way to describe the world as it is today as well as to describe the world as the Scriptures declare it will one day become. Although today we see only the world as it is—fallen, agonizing, anticipating—yet it is one that is harmonious even in death as a result of God entering into the life of every organism down to the very microbial level of existence, to work out a marvelous drama of rebirth and renewal. In doing so, our so-called "imperfect world" yet contains in it the seeds of tomorrow—a marvelous foreshadowing of a world in which God will inevitably fulfill His promise of life everlasting.

And if anyone asks why God didn't provide an easier way to understand the ambiguous statements concerning the ultimate destiny of every living creature on this planet, we only have to recall that God always offers us two ways of interpreting the message of *The Bible*—the way of faith or the way of doubt, the way of hope or the way of cynicism.

In the end, the greatest irony of cynicism is, all that the cynic insists is proof of this world's negativity winds up being the catalyst that produces everything that is ultimately deemed positive. As Jeff Bridges' alien character in the 1984 movie *Starman* observed: "You people are at your best when things are at their worst." If that's true, then everything that the cynical mind is so proud to distance itself from is in fact … everything that makes life worth living.

THIS CONCLUDES *Conquering Cynicism in a Modern Age*. To get the eBook version of this publication, go to *The Lost Stories Channel* at loststorieschannel.com or *Amazon Books*.

Additionally, for those of you who are so inclined, please post a positive review on Amazon so that others might become aware of its valuable contents. Because this book was not published by a conglomerate-style publishing house, we rely more heavily on word-of-mouth to advertise its importance to others who, like yourself, are searching for books like this. Thank you for your support.

BIBLIOGRAPHY

AMBROSE Bierce, *The Cynic's Word Book*, 1906, Doubleday, Page & Company

———. *A Cynic Looks at Life*, 1912, The Neale Publishing Company

Dio Chrysostom, *On Virtue, or Diogenes*, c. 82 to 96 A.D.

Dick Keyes, *Seeing Through Cynicism: A Reconsideration of the Power of Suspicion*, 2006, InterVarsity Press

John Stuart Mill, *An Examination of Sir William Hamilton's Philosophy*, 1865, Longman, Green, Longman, Roberts & Green

———. "The Idea of God in Nature," *Nature, the Utility of Religion and Theism*, 1874, Longman, Green, Reader & Dyer

David Hume, *An Inquiry Concerning Human Understanding*, 1748, J.B. Bebbington

———. *Dialogues Concerning Natural Religion*, 1779, Oxford University

Marcus Tullius Cicero, *On the Nature of the Gods*, 45 B.C.

David Butler, *The Analogy of Religion, Natural and Revealed, to the Constitution and Course of Nature*, 1891, Harper & Brothers

Jean-Jacques Rousseau, *Emile, or Treatise on Education*, 1763, J.M. Dent & Sons

William Paley, *Natural Theology, or Evidences of the Existence and Attributes of the Deity*, 1802, R. Faulder—New Bond-Street

Keith Thomson, *Before Darwin: Reconciling God and Nature*, 2005, Yale University Press

Thomas Paine, *Common Sense*, 1776, R. Bell
———. "Of the Religion of Deism Compared with the Christian Religion," *The Prospect, or View of the Moral World*, 1804
———. The American Crisis, *The Pennsylvania Journal*, 1776
———. *The Age of Reason*, 1794, T. & J. Swords

Jean-Baptiste Dumas, "On the Chemical Statics of Organized Beings," *The London, Edinburgh, and Dublin Philosophical Magazine and Journal of Science*, XLVIII, 3rd Series, 1841

Edward B. Davis, "Robert Boyle, the Bible and Natural Philosophy," *Religions*, June 2023, Vol. 14 Issue 6

Robert Boyle, *Seraphic Love: Some Motives and Incentives to the Love of God*, 1648, Henry Herringman
———. *The Christian Virtuoso*, 1690, Edward Jones

John Ray, *The Wisdom of God Manifested in the Works of Creation*, 1691, Samuel Smith

Peter C. Remien, *The Oeconomy of Nature: Literature and Ecology in the English Renaissance*, 2019, Cambridge University Press

Thomas Burnet, *The Sacred Theory of the Earth*, 1691, R. Norton

Geir Hestmark, "Oeconomia Naturae L.," *Nature*, Vol. 405, 2000

Carl Linnaeus, *The System of Nature*, 1735, Laurentii Salvii
———. *The Economy of Nature*, 1749, Isaac Biberg

Charles Darwin, *The Origin of Species*, 1859, John Murray

Charles H. Pence and Daniel G. Swaim, "The Economy of Nature: The Structure of Evolution in Linnaeus, Darwin and Toward the Extended Synthesis," 2017

Fritjof Capra, *The Web of Life: A New Scientific Understanding of Living Systems*, 1996, Anchor Books

Ernst Haeckel, *Principles of Animal Ecology*, 1866, George Reimer

Michael Lee Cain, William D. Bowman and Sally D. Hacker, *Ecology*, 2014, Palgrave Macmillan

Elizabeth McDuffie, "Ecology and Theology in Dialogue: Death and Resurrection from an Ecological and Theological Perspective," 2010, MA Theses

Lisbet Koerner, *Linnaeus: Nature and Nation*, 1999, Harvard University Press

Adam Gopnik, "Right Again: The Passions of John Stuart Mill," *The New Yorker*, Sep 29, 2008

Jose Harris, "John Stuart Mill," *Oxford Dictionary of National Biography*, Jan 5, 2012

E. Randall Floyd, *The Good, the Bad and the Mad: Some Weird People in American History*, 1990, Barnes & Noble

Roy Morris, *Ambrose Bierce: Alone in Bad Company*, 1999, Oxford University Press

Gregory Claeys, *The Cambridge Companion to Utopian Literature*, 2010, Cambridge University Press

H.D.M. Spence-Jones and Joseph S. Exell, *The Pulpit Commentary*, 1899, Funk & Wagnalls Company

Joseph Benson, *The Benson Commentary*, 1839, T. Mason & G. Lane

Robert Jamieson, Andrew Robert Fausset and David Brown, *Jamieson-Fausset-Brown Bible Commentary*, 1871, S.S. Scranton & Company

Albert Barnes, *Barnes' Notes on The Bible*, 1832, Leavitt, Lord & Company

World History Encyclopedia, 2014, World Book

Wikipedia, Jimmy Wales and Larry Sanger

ABOUT THE AUTHOR

FOR MORE than forty years, W. Kent Smith has immersed himself in the teachings of the greatest biblical scholars of the ages—William Barclay, C.S. Lewis, W. Gene Scott, *et al.* More importantly during that time, he has immersed himself in *The Bible* itself. Add to that, Kent's unique perspective on history, humanity, and life, and the result is a one-of-a-kind take on biblical history and theology.

What that means to you as a fellow truth seeker is a message unhindered by many outmoded traditions of biblical interpretation.

Beholden to no deacon board or school of thought, Kent has remained free to tread where others are unwilling to tread, and because of that, a brand-new view of Scripture has emerged. Not some new revelation, mind you, in the sense of it being above and beyond *The Bible* itself. What we are talking about is a fresh understanding of what Scripture has been saying all along, one that's been hidden in plain sight, waiting for someone to connect the dots, to reveal a picture that's been lying dormant until now.

Kent lives in West Covina, California, an eastern suburb of Los Angeles. He can be contacted at wkent@loststorieschannel.com or lodestarcinema@msn.com.

www.ingramcontent.com/pod-product-compliance
Lightning Source LLC
Chambersburg PA
CBHW060502030426
42337CB00015B/1701